THE TEST

THE TEST

My Life, and the Inside Story of the Greatest Ashes Series

Simon Jones
and Jon Hotten

YELLOW JERSEY PRESS
LONDON

13 5 7 9 10 8 6 4 2

Yellow Jersey Press, an imprint of Vintage
20 Vauxhall Bridge Road,
London SW1V 2SA

Yellow Jersey Press is part of the Penguin Random House group of companies
whose addresses can be found at global.penguinrandomhouse.com

Penguin
Random House
UK

First published in Yellow Jersey in 2015

www.vintage-books.co.uk

A CIP catalogue record for this book is
available from the British Library

ISBN 9780224100274

Printed and bound by Clays Ltd, St Ives Plc

MIX
Paper from
responsible sources
FSC
www.fsc.org   FSC® C018179

Penguin Random House is committed to a sustainable future for
our business, our readers and our planet. This book is made from
Forest Stewardship Council® certified paper

To Justine, Harvey, Charlie, mum and dad, Richard and Math.
Thank you for sticking with me.

Contents

The 2005 Ashes – Teams and nicknames: a handy guide

England

Michael Vaughan – Vaughany

Marcus Trescothick – Tres, Tresco, Banger (love of sausages)

Andrew Strauss – Straussy, Lord Brocket (posh)

Ian Bell – Belly

Kevin Pietersen – Kev, KP

Andrew Flintoff – Fred (as in Flintstone)

Ashley Giles – Gilo

Geraint Jones – Jonah

Matthew Hoggard – Hoggy

Steve Harmison – Harmi

Simon Jones – Jonah, Horse (fast runner)

Paul Collingwood – Colly

The coach: Duncan Fletcher – Fletch

Australia

Ricky Ponting – Punter (love of betting)

Matthew Hayden – Haydos, Buzz (as in Lightyear, used by England only)

Justin Langer – JL, Lang

Damien Martyn – Damo
Simon Katich – Kato
Michael Clarke – Pup (youngster)
Adam Gilchrist – Gilly
Shane Warne – Warnie
Jason Gillespie – Dizzy (surname tie-in)
Brett Lee – Binger (bowls fast)
Glenn McGrath – Pigeon (thin legs)
Mike Kasprowicz – Kasper
Shaun Tait – Wild Thing (unpredictable bowler)

The coach: John Buchanan

Preface

The Australians arrived in England in the summer of 2005 as the winners of eight consecutive Ashes series, meaning that they had held sport's best-known funeral urn for eighteen years, the longest period of dominance by either side since the contest began (England won the first eight series, played between 1882 and 1892).

In addition, Australia were the world's number-one ranked Test team. Since October 1999, they had played in twenty-one series, winning eighteen, drawing two and losing just once, to India in India. Along the way they had won sixteen consecutive Test matches, a world record that demonstrated their commitment to unrelenting, aggressive cricket. In the fifty-over format they had won the World Cup in 1999 and 2003 (and they would win again in 2007).

By contrast, England were emerging from a dark period in the 1990s under a new captain, Michael Vaughan, and an innovative coach, the Zimbabwean Duncan Fletcher. Beginning in March 2004, they had won Test series against West Indies away, and then New Zealand and West Indies in England. Most recently and significantly they had defeated South Africa in South Africa, offering hope that the Ashes series would at least be a more competitive one.

In the early summer of 2005 England won two Tests against Bangladesh before a first meeting with Australia, a one-off T20 international – just the second ever played – at the Rose Bowl in Southampton. England won by the margin of 100 runs in front of a raucous, sell-out crowd.

The two sides next joined Bangladesh in an ODI tri-series that began in shocking fashion for Australia. Having been defeated in a high-scoring warm-up game against Somerset, they lost to Bangladesh in Cardiff, and then to England in Bristol – thanks to a spectacular innings from a new star, Kevin Pietersen. Although they recovered to share the title with England after a tied final at Lord's, and then went on to win the following three-match mini-series 2–1, there were signs that not all was well: the all-rounder Andrew Symonds was dropped after going on a bender before the first Bangladesh game, and their imposing opening batsman, Matthew Hayden, was short of runs and suffering from a shoulder injury.

These were merely early skirmishes, and Australia were well used to the phoney war that accompanied an Ashes series. Their Test side was settled, whereas England found themselves facing a delicate selection decision that meant only two of 100-cap veteran Graham Thorpe, the highly rated Ian Bell and the emerging Kevin Pietersen would make the team. Thorpe missed out, and the sides headed for Lord's in the third week of July for the first of five matches that would be played out over just fifty-three days.

1. Lord's

In which I realise just how good the Aussies are, take a wicket with my first ball, lose a girlfriend in a kiss and tell, and narrowly avoid a punch-up...

Hayden, Langer, Ponting, Martyn, Clarke, Katich, Gilchrist, Lee, Warne, Gillespie, McGrath.

These are the names that Duncan Fletcher writes on the board in a room at the Landmark Hotel. In two days' time, we will play against them at Lord's in the seventy-eighth Ashes series.

England have not won the Ashes since 28 December 1986, when I was eight years and three days old.

I look around the room. We're a young team. Andrew Strauss was nine back then. So was Matthew Hoggard. So was Andrew Flintoff. Steve Harmison was eight. The new guy, Kevin Pietersen, was six. Ian Bell was three. None of us remember England holding the Ashes. Even our captain, Michael Vaughan, was only twelve. We are a generation that has grown up in Australia's shadow.

Since 28 December 1986: defeat. Eighteen years, eight series, four here, four there, forty-three Tests, of which they have won twenty-eight and we have won seven. Eighteen years, eight series, eight defeats.

Fletcher leads the team meeting. His system is, 'The what, the how, the why'. What's the problem? How do we approach it? Why do we do it like that?

How should we be in the field? Create pressure. Keep going, even in a lull. Stick together. Fletcher wants one run out per innings. Then the bowlers only have to take eighteen wickets instead of twenty. How do we take those wickets? Bowl in partnerships. Build pressure. Bat four sessions, score four hundred, bowl them out. When we're batting, Fletcher wants sixty runs from the last three wickets.

Everything works in theory. Everyone wins on paper.

Hayden, Langer, Ponting, Martyn, Clarke, Katich, Gilchrist, Lee, Warne, Gillespie, McGrath.

We look at the names on the board. Duncan Fletcher goes through each one: where to bowl, where not to bowl…

Hayden
5,767 runs at 52.90, 20 centuries, highest score 380.
Look to get a nick from a fourth-stump line; bowl your bouncer on leg stump – he can hook in the air from that position; bowl dot balls – has a big ego and doesn't like being tied down; set a straight catcher on the drive – can hit in the air through mid-off/extra cover. Drag him wide of off with length balls and then look for LBW with inswinger.

Langer

6,607 runs at 46.52, 21 centuries, highest score 250.

Bowl an early bouncer; put a man close in on the drive – can confuse him; use a short-leg for swing and turn – can inside edge onto his pad; spin outlet shot is loft over mid-on.

Ponting

6,950 runs at 56.50, 22 centuries, highest score 257.

Wants to impose himself early – can nick off to the drive ball, also try surprise yorker; straight ball for LBW – can play across his pad; flick in air through midwicket.

Martyn

3,947 runs at 51.25, 12 centuries, highest score 165.

TOO – top of off.

Clarke

669 runs at 49.81, 2 centuries, highest score 155.

Attack the stumps – look for bowled or nick behind on the drive; run-out candidate early; can drive uppishly through cover/midwicket; short stuff on off-stump line (poor puller from there).

Katich

975 runs at 44.31, 2 centuries, highest score 125.

Push ball across him, get him driving for a nick. Walks across stumps – early yorker.

Gilchrist

4,452 runs at 55.65, 15 centuries, highest score 204.
Nick behind from off stump or just outside – full ball; hits back of a length balls uppishly; go around the wicket and cramp him for room; keep a gully in.

We go through the lower order too – Warne and Lee can be dangerous hitters; we need to force them back with short stuff, vary our pace, try to nick them off driving. Gillespie and McGrath are real tail-enders – we should be able to knock them over with some good basic principles.

We talk about their bowling. Between them, Warne and McGrath have 1,081 Test wickets. Individually they have taken more Test wickets than any English bowler ever in the history of the game.[1]

Duncan Fletcher looks up at us and says, 'I want to hear from some of the young guys.'

I don't say anything. No one says anything. None have played against the Australian Test team before, with the exception of me. I bowled seven overs at Brisbane in the first Test of the 2002–3 series before I ruptured my anterior cruciate ligament when my knee got jammed in the turf when I was trying to prevent a boundary and I couldn't walk for seven months.

The silence goes on. Then Kevin Pietersen, the new bloke,

---

[1] We were the least experienced side by a long way. Australia's team for Lord's had a combined 730 caps, more than double our 325. Their batsman had scored 94 Test hundreds, ours had made 37. Australia's bowlers had taken 1,468 Test wickets between them, we had taken 551.

says: 'Warnie…I play with him at Hampshire. You can't let him just bowl at you. He's a legend, and he'll try to bully you, but if you go at him hard, he can go into his shell.'

Shane Warne has won six Ashes series in his career, as well as two World Cups. Since he's been in the Australian team, they've only ever lost one series, to India in India.

'Good,' says Duncan Fletcher. 'That's good, Kev. Anyone else?'

I'm back in my room when the telephone rings. I pick up. It's a girl called Terri.

'Hi, Simon, do you remember me?'

I do. Three weeks ago, after the one-day international at Headingley. We'd gone out to celebrate the win, and I'd ended up hammered in a student disco. Terri was a model. We'd got talking, and I took her back to the hotel. I'm not proud of it, because I've got a lovely girlfriend called Kim, who I've been with for four years. Anyhow, we get back to the room and I'm so far gone, I make Terri a cup of tea, give her some Pringles from the minibar and collapse on the bed unconscious.

'Yeah, yeah, Terri…of course I remember…'

'Well that night, did you use a condom?'

'What do you mean? You know that nothing happened, Terri.'

'Oh, okay then,' she says and hangs up.

That's odd, I think, and forget all about it.

*

Fletcher tells me the day before the game that I'm in the eleven. I'm nervous but at least I'll get a decent night's sleep. It had taken me a year to get fit after Brisbane, and, for a long while after that, the fourth bowling spot was between me and another young, not-quite-established quick Jimmy Anderson. Often, they'd wait until the morning of the match and see what the weather was like before they decided between us. If it was cloudy, Jimmy played because it might swing. If it was sunny, I'd play because I could reverse it. It was stupid. The weather could change in a couple of hours.

They thought I was a one-trick pony with the reverse swing but I knew I wasn't. My third Test wicket was Sehwag. The next was Laxman. I've knocked over Justin Langer in Brisbane, Brian Lara in Kingston, Chanderpaul and Gayle in Port of Spain, Fleming and McCullum at Lord's, Kallis and Pollock in Port Elizabeth, Rudolph and Amla in Cape Town, AB de Villiers in Durban and Centurian... You need more than one trick to get players like that out.

It wasn't until last winter and South Africa that it felt as if I'd won the battle with Jimmy. In the first Test at Port Elizabeth Vaughan didn't bowl me for two and a half sessions. I was walking around the boundary thinking, 'The captain doesn't fancy me here... He doesn't trust me...'

Then I got four for him in their second innings and I was in: fifteen wickets at 26.66 in a series that we won, a series where our attack came together. Harmison and Hoggard with the new ball. Harmison off, Flintoff on. Hoggard off, me on. Ashley Giles to hold an end with his slow left armers. We bowl as a team, bowl to our plans. Work the batsmen out. Work the batsmen over. Fast stuff, short stuff, seam and swing, skill and persistence. Twenty wickets a match is our job – eighteen if Fletch gets his run-outs...

Day one

I leave the Landmark early, out onto the backstreets of Marylebone, the morning traffic backing up, the day already warm under the low grey summer clouds. A bowl-first kind of feeling. It's 8.15 when I get to the ground and there's a long queue of MCC members waiting for the Grace Gates to open so that they can race to the Pavilion and secure a seat. It's quite a sight when it happens. 'The Donkey Derby' the players call it, because there are usually a couple of fallers amongst the field. When you see them on TV, dozing in the sun in their egg and bacon ties on the white benches by the Pavilion gates, you don't realise that MCC membership doesn't guarantee a view of the game. All they get is admittance to the Pavilion – hence the thrills and spills of the Derby.

Today, the first day of the Ashes, already feels different. There will be no dozing on the benches today. So many members will arrive that the Pavilion doormen will be forced to operate a 'one in, one out' policy.

The players' dressing rooms are up two flights of wide stairs, which, apart from the actual entrance to the rooms and the showers across the corridor, are open to the members too. Except when we are in the dressing rooms or the showers or the players' dining room, the members will be there too, milling about. Applause and banter if you've done well.

7

Heavy silence if you've not. It makes the atmosphere unique, and some players find it hard to get used to, but I love it here, bloody love it at Lord's. I made my England debut here. I took my first Test wicket here. I love the ground itself, with its slope that runs from one side to the other. I love the Nursery End, where I usually bowl and where the slope helps me to shape the ball away from the right-handed batsmen. And I love the home dressing room, which is large and more modern than you'd think, with lots of space, even if you're changing next to Flintoff, who chucks his bag down, throws his dirty kit on the floor and leaves it there for all five days, festering.

My spot is just inside the door, to the right, against the wall. Flintoff and all of his shit will be opposite, with his great mate Harmi next to him. KP's just the other side of the door to me. Bell is near him. Gilo's next to Bell. The coach is at the back, a man apart...

Dressing rooms are private places, tribal places, places with rituals and codes of their own, closed to the outsider. Once you get a seat, you always change there, day after day, match after match, year after year. It can be hard when you first come in and you don't really have a spot of your own and you don't know how to act or how everything works, but I feel at home now, and we are a young team, young and welcoming, with no cliques and no jealousy, no scars and few defeats.

An hour or so later I have warmed up, had a bit of a massage and a chat with Troy Cooley, who is the specialist fast-bowling coach, a close friend and a big supporter of mine. I owe a lot to Troy. He's Australian, but this summer he will be English.

He will plot the Australian downfall, press his thumb on their sore spots. By the end of the summer, the Australians will be wishing that Troy Cooley worked for them.

The time seems to stand still and then accelerate. One minute it is half past nine and the next Vaughan is out there and he has won the toss and put the Australians in to bat and we're walking down the stairs through the packed Pavilion, and it hits me, hits us all, that this is on, and it's different, very different from any feeling I've had at Lord's before. The members aren't just clapping and chatting, they're roaring and shouting as we walk past, even in the Long Room, and I understand it's because for the first time in a long time, the first time in eighteen years, they think that this is an England team with a chance of beating the Australians, beating the greatest ongoing dynasty that has ever played the game.

Through the Long Room we go, studs clacking on the wooden floor, the members forming a small tunnel that we just about fit through, out of the doors and onto the concrete, through the gate and onto the pitch. Vaughan calls us together in a huddle for a few last words as the rest of the crowd gets its first sight of us and starts to clap and roar too.

Right behind us are the Australian openers, Langer and Hayden. When they walk down the stairs and through the crush in the Long Room there are no claps for them, no cheers for them, not today. Instead there's just a tense quiet that I wouldn't want to walk through.

Today, it will be Harmison at the Pavilion End and Hoggard at the Nursery End. I'm at backward square leg for a mistimed hook. I want an early touch of the ball, that brand-new

Duke's cherry, so rich and dark it's almost brown, just the way we like it.

An English ball for an English day.

Hayden is the non-striker. He leans on his bat, chewing gum. He's a huge guy and likes to belt the ball hard. He's got close-set eyes and a giant chest. Buzz Lightyear, we call him. Never a backward step from Buzz – unless he's trying to take gully's head off with one of his meaty square cuts. He has flayed the England attack for years, especially in Australia, but this summer in the one-dayers we have got inside his head and he hasn't scored any runs. We've bowled tight lines and drawn him forwards, with no room to swing those massive arms. Hoggy has done him with late inswing, and it has brought doubt, even in a man like Haydos.

At the striker's end is his little mate, Langer. Justin's the opposite of Hayden physically, small and light on his feet, but he's got a black belt in karate, and, like a lot of short guys, he's ultra-aggressive with the bat, and with the chat sometimes too. 'The eye of the tiger', he calls it.

Hayden and Langer hit attacks hard, set the tone for the Australian killing machine, and because they're both left-handed and require different lengths from the bowlers, they can be a nightmare: boundaries flying everywhere, fifty on the board before you can blink, the ball already looking as if a dog's been chewing it, and that big juggernaut rolling right towards you.

But today that will not happen, because Steve Harmison has his rhythm from the Pavilion End. He is rapid and he is aggressive, pounding the ball into the pitch from nine feet high, making it rear alarmingly from a length. With the second ball of his first over he hits Langer on the arm, and the physio runs on. With the fifth ball of his first over, he forces Hayden into a panicky fend that flies off his glove for four.

All of a sudden Hayden and Langer are looking at one another and saying, 'Okay, this is on...'

With the sixth ball of his second over, Harmison almost cuts Langer in half. With the fourth ball of his third he hits Hayden on the helmet.

In between, Hayden and Langer are going for their shots, fighting back, hitting boundaries. Half an hour flies by. Australia are 30-0 from the first seven overs. Then from the last ball of the eighth, Hoggard gets Hayden where he wants him at last, coming forward and trying to force a full ball that is swinging beautifully and late and through the gate. The off stump is knocked back.

Lord's goes nuts, a great, deep-throated roar followed by extended applause. Hayden out exactly to plan, only twelve runs to his name, and all of the doubts and the fears from the one-dayers still there.

I can't wait to get on to bowl, can't bloody wait, keep looking at the skipper, but now that Hoggy's nabbed Haydos, he'll get a couple more overs.

Ricky Ponting walks onto the ground. Ponting the skipper, Ponting the legend, the talismanic number three who drives their batting along with his murderous pull shot and his famous straight drive, Ponting who never loses, not to England, not in the Ashes...

From the fourth ball of the tenth over, Harmison digs one in and Ponting goes for his pull, but this time the ball doesn't fly from the centre of his bat, this time it rises past his front elbow and smashes into the sidepiece of his helmet as he tries to twist his head out of the way. The impact forces the grille into his cheek.

No one goes up to him to ask if he's okay. No one says a word to Ricky Ponting. He glares back down the pitch at Langer and gets ready to take guard, and then he feels it, the trickle of blood running down his face from underneath his helmet, staining the fresh white collar of his new Australian shirt.

The physio comes out again, this time to patch Ponting up. The captain bats on. He takes part of an over from Hoggard. Langer takes the rest. Australia get to fifty. It feels as though something is happening every ball.

Ponting hits the first delivery of Harmison's sixth over for four, and Harmi tries to drag him wide with the next, tries to get him driving, but Ponting leaves it alone. He defends the next two, but then Harmi pulls him out wide again, wide of the off stump where the drive can be dangerous, especially when the ball is lifting and you're not really set, and Ponting nicks it to Strauss. The talisman is out, walking back to the Pavilion with blood on his collar and nine runs against his name.

Harmison comes off and Flintoff replaces him. I look over at Vaughany, who rolls his shoulders at me. I get warmed up. Can't wait, can't bloody wait to bowl at Justin Langer and Damien Martyn, can't wait to bowl at the Nursery End in an Ashes Test, blood on the wicket and the ball in my hand...

But before I can, Freddie pounds in at the Pavilion End, adrenaline pumping, and the fourth ball of his first over flies at

Langer's head. He tries to pull, but the ball's on him too quickly and it takes the shoulder of his bat and arcs high into the air at square leg, where Harmison holds the catch easily.

The roar is another huge one, eighteen years of defeat behind it. Eighteen years of waiting for a morning like this, with the Australians on the rack.

I can't wait, can't bloody wait, and finally, after Langer has walked off and Clarke has walked in, the ball is in my hand, still dark, and with a deep blush on one side. Perfect, just perfect. Damien Martyn is on strike. Unlike Hayden, Langer and Ponting, Martyn is a touch player, free scoring and elegant, never hurried. No glaring weaknesses to go for.

I stand at the end of my run, breathing deeply. 'Just hit your length as hard as you can,' I tell myself, and in I go. Just before my delivery stride I think what I always think: 'Don't bowl a bad ball...' Not a bad one. Not here, not now, at Lord's in an Ashes Test, with my parents in the stands and Australia on 66-3.

I hit the crease and it comes out not badly but well, on a good length a hair or two outside off stump and as if in a dream, Damien Martyn is stepping out elegantly towards it, his bat away from his pad, the ball curling just a little further down the slope, the slope that has fooled so many. It fools Damien Martyn too, fools him into chasing that ball and feathering an edge through to Geraint Jones, an edge that makes such a noise that nobody could possibly miss it, and I'm exploding with joy, a feeling I can't really describe other than to say it is all-consuming, and then the roar is going up again and the lads are all around me, rubbing the top of my head, and the unbeatable Australians are 66-4 at Lord's.

Unreal. Just unreal.

As I go back to my mark, Rudi Koertzen, the South African umpire who is standing at the Nursery End, says, 'Don't do that again.'

'Do what?'

'Turn away from me before you appeal.'

'But it was a clear edge. Everyone heard it...'

'Doesn't matter. The rules have changed. You have to appeal for it.'

I look up to the stands to the spot where I know my parents are, and I smile.

Simon Katich comes in and leaves his first ball, then clips the second to long leg for a single. I bowl to Michael Clarke, three away-swingers in a row, trying to get him driving. He thick-edges the first for four through third man and leaves the next two.

In my second over I'm pumped and bowl a wide and then a half volley that Katich drives for four. My next is tighter. Clarke gets a single. Lunch is coming. Lunch on day one of the Ashes at Lord's and we are still all over them, still on top. Flintoff keeps Katich on strike at his end, so I get a full over at Clarke. I want to drag him across the crease, so ball one is on the line of the stumps, but I push it a little and it jags well down the leg side. The next one starts on off stump and shapes away down the hill, so he leaves it alone. I try for the same thing again but get too straight and Clarke is onto it quickly, whipping it up the hill to the midwicket boundary. Fuck. *Come on Si, get him straighter, get him driving.*

I hit the pitch hard with the next one and maybe because he's pumped from the boundary Clarke does drive hard and misses, and the ball buzzes past the outside edge.

He won't do that again, so I start the next on off stump and it comes up the hill a little, up the hill a little too much for Michael Clarke, and it rips into his pads. All of us, Geraint, the slips, me, look at Rudi Koertzen, bellow at him, scream and screech and beseech Rudi Koertzen until, finally, slowly, his arm begins to raise and his finger goes up and Michael Clarke is done, gone, and Australia are 87-5 with one over to come before lunch.

After the break, Adam Gilchrist makes 26 before he nicks one from Flintoff and is caught. Shane Warne makes 28 before Harmison bowls him behind his legs. Simon Katich makes 27 before he mistimes a pull-shot and Geraint Jones catches a skier. Brett Lee makes three before Harmison rockets a short ball between his bat and his body and Aleem Dar gives him out. Jason Gillespie makes a single before he walks into a full one from Harmison and Aleem Dar gives him out too. Glenn McGrath has hit a single boundary and Australia are all out for 190 in 40.2 overs and 209 minutes. The crowd roar us from the field, the members in the Long Room are laughing and shouting and patting our backs, and we are all buzzed, electrified by this heightened beginning that has seen Australia score at almost five runs per over despite the wickets clattering.

The bowling unit has done its job but we keep a lid on it once we reach the dressing room, because the batsmen have to pad up and prepare themselves to go out there and face Glenn McGrath and Jason Gillespie, Brett Lee and Shane Warne with enough time for five overs before tea on day one of an Ashes Test.

Glenn McGrath is magic against England. He's magic against England *in* England, and most of all, he's magic against England in England at Lord's. In 1997, bowling from the Pavilion End, he took 8-38 and 1-65, and in 2001 he took 5-54 and 3-60. In all, 17 wickets at 12.76.

Glenn McGrath has played 109 times for Australia and in those matches he has taken 499 Test wickets. Only three men in the history of the game have got to 500 Test match wickets, and one of them is Shane Warne.[2] Now Glenn McGrath has the ball in his hands at the Pavilion End at Lord's once more. There's time to bowl three overs before tea and everyone in the ground knows what's coming, everyone knows what Glenn McGrath will try to do. Marcus Trescothick and Andrew Strauss know it too, but they resist him and they resist Brett Lee from the Nursery End and we reach the break intact at 10-0.

But then it happens, then it comes. With the first ball after tea, under the gentle afternoon sun, McGrath takes the wicket of Trescothick, who tries to turn a straight ball to leg and nicks it to Langer at third slip. With the fifth ball after

---

[2] Ten years on from the series, Glenn McGrath and Courtney Walsh of West Indies are still the only fast bowlers to have gone past 500 Test wickets, with 563 and 519 respectively. India's champion leg spinner Anil Kumble took his 500th Test wicket in 2006, and is the last bowler of any kind to have passed the mark. Kumble ended his career with a round 600, leaving only Shane Warne (708) and Muttiah Muralitharan (800) above him on the list.

tea, he takes the wicket of Strauss, who edges low to Warne at first slip. With the second ball of his seventh over he takes the wicket of Michael Vaughan, who is bowled by a ball that keeps low and hits halfway up his off stump. With the third ball of his eighth over he takes the wicket of Ian Bell, who is bowled by an unplayable one that pitches on off stump and jags back to take the inside edge and clip the bails. With the first ball of his ninth over he takes the wicket of Andrew Flintoff, who is bowled by a ball that lands on the seam and nips down the slope, goes through the gate and lifts out the off stump.

At the end of the seventeenth over, we are 25-5, and McGrath has bowling figures of 9-4-11-5.

Magic against England. Magic at Lord's, where it always happens. Five hundred and four Test match wickets – only the fourth man in history to do it, and two of them are playing in this game. On the dressing-room television, Ritchie Benaud says, 'I don't think I've ever seen McGrath bowl a better spell.'

The Test match is moving at a bewildering pace. It has a momentum of its own that each side can ride for a while but neither seems to be able to control. Fifteen wickets have fallen since eleven o'clock, fifteen wickets in fifty-six overs.

When a collapse like this happens, the dressing room is a chaotic place. Lads are coming back after being dismissed and having to deal with their disappointment. Lads who are waiting to bat get edgier and edgier as their time comes. No one is sure when they should pad up. There's kit everywhere. Some watch from the balcony. Some watch on the television. Some don't watch. Some are swearing. Some are quiet. Duncan Fletcher says nothing. Vaughany takes off his pads and sits down.

Kevin Pietersen and Geraint Jones are batting. Kev is playing his first Test innings. Geraint is short of runs.

Gillespie bowls a maiden to Kev. They have drinks. McGrath bowls a maiden to Jonah. Gillespie starts the next with a short wide one and Kev absolutely smokes it through cover for his first boundary in Test cricket. In the next over, Jonah hits McGrath for four. In the over after that, he drives Gillespie for another.

McGrath has bowled twelve in a row and he must be getting tired now, despite all the adrenaline, and the stamina he has built up over years of bowling fast for Australia. In his next, Jonah hits him to the boundary again and Ponting finally takes him off.

Jonah hits Gillespie for four, Kev hits Brett Lee for another and Geraint smacks yet another, then Kev whacks Gillespie through square leg, and instead of wickets falling it's boundaries that are coming, and very quickly we double the score. Kev really gets into Gillespie, just like he did at Bristol in the one-dayer. He whistles him for a boundary through midwicket to bring up the fifty partnership and then he's waiting for the inevitable short one next ball; he sees it so early that he cracks it hard through mid-on, and the crowd are going nuts here, totally caught up in it, and we are too, the mood in the dressing room lifting with every shot.

Ponting can't keep Gillespie on after that, so he's off and it's Shane Warne from the Nursery End with maybe four or five overs of this mad day left. Warne to Pietersen, Shane to Kev, legend to debutant. Mates at Hampshire. I think about the team meeting at the Landmark: *'You've got to push him back...'*

The first ball drifts and spins and takes the pad. Warne shouts for leg before, not because he thinks it's out but because Warnie works an umpire like no one else on earth – he'll be in Koertzen's ear right away, and in Kev's...

'That was close, Rudi...You must have thought about that...'

Placing doubt. Placing fear.

The next one lands outside leg stump and Kev pads it away. Warne goes, 'Ooh.' So does Gilchrist. Gilly sings his eternal song: 'Bowling, Warnie...'

Kev blocks out the next four okay but right away, Warne has changed the momentum, subtly altered the feeling in the ground. There are two or three overs to go, depending on how quickly the Australians turn around between them, and suddenly they *are* turning round, and Brett Lee is absolutely steaming in and the first delivery of his next over is a 90 mph throat ball that Geraint Jones does well to glove. It flies high in the air for Gilchrist to catch and we're six wickets down. Ashley Giles walks in and somehow keeps out an inswinging yorker first up, then he ducks a bouncer, then he edges a boundary through gully and pushes another through mid-on. Warne bowls the next over quickly to give Lee one more, and with the final ball of the day he strangles Gilo, who tries to play a leg glance and edges through to Gilchrist. Well, that day was only ever going to end one way...

Later I go for dinner, then to the bar at the Landmark and have a few beers, but I can't relax, can't sleep, can't think anything other than that tomorrow I will bat and bowl against Australia in the Ashes at Lord's.

Sleepless. Helpless. This is Test cricket. This is what it is, and this is what it does.

Australia 190 all out, Langer 40; Harmison 5-43, SP Jones 2-48. England 92-7, Pietersen 28 not out; McGrath 5-21, Lee 2-35.

Day two

It's warm and cloudy in north-west London and I'm already padded up when Kev walks out with Matthew Hoggard to start the second day. Fletcher likes Hoggard to go nine, especially when there's a top-order batter still in, because Hoggy's got a decent defence and he's a tough Yorkie who can take a little rough stuff from the quick bowlers. Fletch isn't bothered whether Harmison or I go ten because we both like to swing the bat and we're probably much of a muchness. Harmi wants it, and eleven doesn't worry me.

One of the best things that Fletch has done is bring in Batting Buddies. It's a system that Steve Waugh invented, where each of the tail is given a specialist batsman who'll work with them to improve their batting. Mine is Marcus Trescothick, which is perfect because we're both lefties. Tres has a wide stance and his method is astonishingly simple. He just watches the ball and swings his hands through it. When you see slo-mo replays of him batting, his eyes are huge and wide as the ball comes down. I think he's a genius. He can kill any bowler, any attack, and he has done, all over the world. He can't show me how to bat like him, but he can make the most of what I've got. I once got 46 from twelve deliveries for Glamorgan against Yorkshire at Scarborough, so there's something to work with.

Fletch wants the tail to be there while sixty runs are made. At 92-7 we need all of those and more.

Ricky Ponting knows it, and this morning, Ricky Ponting is not pissing about.

Ricky Ponting, who has stitches in his face where Harmison hit him yesterday.

Ricky Ponting, who will have all of Australia on his back if he messes this up.

Shane Warne starts from the Nursery End, with Kev on strike, a short-leg in. Right away there's another huge shout for LBW, and Warnie's there, chuntering away to the umpire, to Hoggy, to KP, spreading doubt, spreading fear. Kev gets a single off the last ball of the over.

Glenn McGrath starts from the Pavilion End. His first ball is a fraction wide and Kev creams it through backward point for four. He takes a single from the next, leaving Hoggy with four to face. McGrath tries him with three wide ones, which he leaves, and a short one, which he ducks.

A few overs pass. The morning settles down under heavy skies. Then Warne gets Hoggy on strike and he ties him down with a few at the stumps before throwing one out wider and, before he can stop himself, Hoggy goes for the cut and Hayden parries the fast-moving edge and then grabs the rebound. Warne has his first wicket of the series.

Harmi goes in and I feel the nerves and the adrenaline kick up as he does. I'm next, and the moment could come at any time, with Shane Warne at the Nursery End and Glenn McGrath at the Pavilion End, these legends of the game...

But before it can happen, KP decides that there's no margin in blocking now and instead launches an astonishing assault on Glenn McGrath. First he hits him straight down the ground for four, the ball cracking off his bat with a rifle report. McGrath gives him the teapot.

Kev gets to the pitch of the next one and puts it into the Pavilion seats as if he's facing some net bowler on a flat track in Delhi. McGrath looks really fucked off now, but instead of going short, he double-bluffs and goes line and length and Kev slaughters it through cover to get to fifty in his first Test knock. The dressing room is filled with applause and laughter, no one quite believing what they've just seen. Even the Australians are clapping, and they don't usually bother applauding English fifties. My nerves have turned to excitement – I want to get out there too, to be part of this, because it's pure theatre, pure magic.

Warnie has the ball, and you can see from ninety yards away that he's in Kev's ear. 'Come on buddy, put me in the stands, too...'

Kev hits the first one to cover. No run. Warne throws the next ball up, an invitation, a challenge, and Kev mistimes a drive. No run. Warne throws the next one up and Kev takes him on again: this time it goes into orbit and comes down somewhere over the other side of St John's Wood. Six more.

'You've got to push him back...'

The battle is on now. Neither is going to back off. The next ball is another dipping leg spinner and Kev smacks it high into the warm air above the stands, so high that Damien Martyn has time to sprint flat out for twenty yards and somehow hold the catch. The noise in the ground is like the air being slowly let from a balloon, but I barely hear it because I'm taking the famous walk from the players' balcony back through the dressing room, onto the landing and down the stairs, into the Long Room where my studs clack on the boards and the noise and cheers for Kevin's innings are bloody loud even though he's not off the field yet. He gives me a little grin as we pass each other and suddenly I'm out through the gate and onto the soft green grass of the most famous cricket ground on earth to face Shane Warne and Glenn McGrath in an Ashes Test.

It's quite a moment, quite a thing, when you're twenty-four years old and having the greatest time of your life.

Kev and I have different bat sponsors, but he's given me one of his bats and it's an absolute gun. I've peeled off his Woodworm stickers and put on my Puma ones and it's in my hands as Harmi takes a single from Warne's next ball and then I take guard to face the great man for the first time.

It feels almost unreal, looking down the pitch at him, but there's not long to worry about it because Warne's approach to the crease is one of the shortest in the game. Just a couple of steps at walking pace before he's into his action. All of his power comes from the rotation of his shoulders and the rip that his strong wrist and thick fingers give the ball as he drags them down its sides. I have a slight advantage, being a left-hander, in that his stock delivery will turn into me rather than away, but it's thin consolation because he has a hundred tricks and he's probably the cleverest, most street-smart bowler in the world.

Most of all, he is a master of the psychological side of cricket, where the true game is played. He watches everything you do, and he misses nothing. Do you walk quickly to the wicket or slowly? Do you look down at the ground or up at the sky? How loudly do you ask for your guard? Is your voice wobbling? Is your throat dry? Are you licking your lips? Do you call the umpire by his name? How do you stand? How do you grip the bat?

Warne can process all of this information in an instant, and understand what it means. Then he starts to bowl at you. And he starts to talk to you. Or maybe he starts to talk about you...to Gilly or to Punter, or to the umpire. He is working everyone, all the time. It's an act of drama and an act of magic, of illusion and skill and of deep knowledge of the game.

He throws the first one outside my off stump and I get some of KP's bat on it and I'm away with a single. No respite though because that's the end of the over and now it's Glenn McGrath from the Pavilion End.

McGrath's run-up curves slightly, and he's tall and angular, the ball emerging from a sharp jumble of knees and elbows. When he started out in Test cricket he could bowl almost ninety miles per hour but now he's down at about 84–85 clicks. It's all he needs though because his control of line and length is absolute – Ponting estimates McGrath may bowl four or five loose deliveries *a day* – and he bangs the pitch hard and hits the seam, allowing the natural variations of bounce and movement to do the rest.

Glenn likes to chunter too but it's just swearing. He tries me out with a little width and I take a swing at it and hit him through cover for four.

'You fucking useless ****.'

I smile. He says something else that I don't quite hear. We

24

both know what the next ball will be and I'm ducking almost before he lets it go. McGrath's got a nasty bouncer – it's much quicker than his stock ball and it seems to skid on from a pretty full length. The next one is short too, and I swing at it but miss by miles. He swears again and goes short again and I think better of it and leave it alone. I can hear my heart in my ears.

Ponting takes off Warne and brings on Lee and he's at 90 mph right away, no warm-up, no looseners, just these rockets that sear down at Steve Harmison. Lee's only 5 mph quicker than McGrath, but it makes all the difference: there's just no time to change your mind or change your shot or get out of trouble if you get yourself into it. The saving grace is that Lee's action is so pure that you see the ball all the way from his hand, which gives you maybe a millisecond more to deal with what's coming. We run a single. I take block.

Don't get injured, Si. Don't get hit...

These are the first thoughts in my mind as he comes in. Not because I'm afraid, but because a broken hand or a busted rib would stop me from bowling, keep me out of the Ashes.

Be positive. No point in the scoreboard staying still – we're a few overs into day two, not the end of day five. He digs one in and I stay leg side of it and get it up and over cover for two.

Stand still and watch the ball, like Tres says.

I get a good look at the next one and it screams off the thick edge of KP's bat and goes for four to third man. The next one feels even quicker but the scoop over cover works again, and we run three.

We get a few more singles. Then I carve McGrath on the bounce to third man. I look up at the scoreboard: 146-9.

Ponting takes off Lee and brings on Warne. Harmi walks down the wicket to his first ball and lofts it for four over mid-off as if he's Brian Lara. We're both laughing because we know that the Australians will be hating this; numbers ten and eleven eating into their slim lead, the bowlers frustrated, Hayden and Langer on edge, not knowing when they're going to bat.

Then Ricky Ponting pulls a fast one by taking McGrath off and changing Lee to the Pavilion End. His first ball to Harmi is full and straight, and Harmi tries to get under it and loft it to the boundary but the ball hits low on the bat and spoons up to Martyn at mid-off and it's all over. We trail by 35. The last three wickets have put on 63. Fletch can write that one in his notebook.

Thirty-five runs can be a lot or a little, can mean nothing or everything. For a couple of hours, while Australia are losing Justin Langer for six, run out by Kevin Pietersen, and Matthew Hayden for 34, bowled by Andrew Flintoff, and Ricky Ponting for 42,[3] cutting to point off Hoggy; while Australia are 100-3 and only 135 ahead, 35 runs means that we are still alive, still in the game.

But while I get Michael Clarke to hit a simple one to cover when he's made only 21 and Kev drops it, while a couple of other chances go to ground, while Damien Martyn makes 65 and Clarke gets 91 and Simon Katich gets 67; while their score

---

[3] Forty-two would remain Ricky Ponting's highest Test score at Lord's, the best he managed in eight innings at the home of cricket. Sachin Tendulkar's highest score at Lord's in Test cricket was 37, and Brian Lara's 54 – meaning that the three greatest batsmen of the age had a single half-century between them at the game's most famous ground. As players we all want to get our name on the Honours Board, and it's strange that none of these three has.

goes from 100-3 to 275-5, and their lead goes from 135 to 310; while Australia reach stumps at 279-7, ahead by 314 despite losing Shane Warne to the last ball of the day, 35 runs look as if they are going to mean very little to Australia, or to us.

England 155 all out, Pietersen 57; McGrath 5-53, Lee 3-47, Warne 2-19. Australia second innings 279-7, Clarke 91, Martyn 65; Harmison 2-35.

Day three

Back to the hotel, back to the Landmark, dinner and drinks with my girlfriend Kim, but it's hard to relax, hard to think about anything other than 314 runs and four more wickets to take, four more wickets that we need pronto, because success-ful run chases of more than 300 in the fourth innings of Test matches at Lord's come along about once a century. We know it and Australia know it. They know that they've almost broken our backs in this game, broken us on the wheel, that unless we knock them over very quickly and then bat like gods, we're one-nil down. One-nil down again in the Ashes, the Ashes that we haven't won for eighteen years.

The day comes slowly. I wake up early, get to the ground early, get through my warm-ups and drills and massage, but the omens are there in the first ball of the day which Brett Lee swipes through third man for four, and we never quite dispel them, not when Gilo runs out Lee with a direct hit a few overs later, or when – finally, with the last ball of my thirteenth over and the eighty-ninth over of the Australian second innings – I bowl Jason Gillespie, or when, a couple of overs after lunch, I catch Simon Katich at third man from the bowling of Steve Harmison.

Because instead of knocking Australia over quickly and chasing a few more than 300, we have been kept out there for a hundred overs and they lead by 420, with five sessions left to bowl us out.

It's at times like this that you feel the great weight of Test cricket, how oppressive it can be, how its timescales extend your agony and turn the small margins and fleeting moments of loss into a defeat that looks from the outside to be one-sided and overwhelming. It is the ultimate game of 'what ifs', except you can never allow yourself to think that way. Instead you must live in the moment, never looking back, always looking forward, always keeping yourself afloat with the hope that the next ball, the next over, the next innings, the next game, brings.

It takes 26.3 overs for that great weight of runs to cause a crack. Tres and Straussy bat beautifully until then, scoring 80 together until Brett Lee bangs one in at more than 90 mph and it hurries Straussy into a cramped pull-shot that pops the ball gently into the air and has Lee sprinting and diving and rolling to hold a wonderful catch. Strauss goes for 37. Trescothick bangs Warne for a couple of boundaries but then Warnie does him with a quicker one and he's caught at slip by Matthew Hayden for 44. He does Ian Bell with his quicker one too, leg before to Rudi Koertzen's slow finger of death, and then Brett Lee cleans up Vaughany with a ball that pitches on middle and then moves enough to uproot the off stump. The slide becomes a crash when Warne persuades Freddie to try to cut a straight one and Gilchrist takes the catch.

Kev and Jonah get through to the close, Kev still creaming Warnie all over Lord's – *'You've got to push him back...'* – but it's over and we know it. Five wickets left and two days still to bat.

Australia 384 all out, Clarke 91, Katich 67; Harmison 3-54. England 156-5, Pietersen 42 not out; Warne 3-42. England trail by 264.

I'm in my room at the Landmark on the Saturday night. Kim's in the bedroom. I'm in the bathroom. The phone goes. I pick it up. It's Andrew Walpole. He's our press officer.

'Jonah, I'm sorry but there's a story about you in the *Sunday People* tomorrow, and there's nothing I can do to stop it.'

'What sort of story?'

'Do you know a girl called Terri?'

Things fall into place.

'Yeah, I know her.'

'Did she call you the other day?'

'Yeah, she did.'

'Well she was calling from the newspaper office. They were listening in. You confirmed that she came to your room. They're going with it.'

'Andrew, nothing happened...'

'Sorry mate. At least you know it's coming.'

I tell Kim. I explain that nothing happened. She leaves

anyway. I've got a bit of form in these matters, something that happened in the West Indies...

I get a call from Matthew Hoggard.

'What's going on, mate?'

Hoggy's wife Sarah is big pals with Kim. Kim and Sarah are out at a bar. Hoggy takes me to the hotel bar. We drink two or three beers.

'Mate, I swear nothing happened.'

'I know. I believe you. Sarah believes you too.'

I wake at six the next morning because Kim is hitting me over the head with a copy of the *Sunday People*. They've run the story over a spread. On one side is a picture of Terri in her underwear. On the other is a picture of Kim standing in the street smoking. They are both beautiful girls but one looks good and one doesn't. It's hard on Kim.

I know what I have to say.

'Look Kim, nothing happened. You can believe me, or you can believe that paper, but this is the most important summer of my life, and I can't have anything distracting me.'

It sounds hard, but I realise even as I'm saying it that this is how things have to be. Fletcher gets to hear of what's happened and he asks Matt Maynard to walk with me from the Landmark to the ground and judge my state of mind.

'So, Jonah...' he says.

Matt and I have known each other for a long time at Glamorgan. I hold his stare.

'Mate, I'm fine. One hundred per cent. Nothing is going to get in the way of this.'

He doesn't need to say anything else.

When we get to the dressing room, there's a cup of tea and a tube of Pringles waiting by my kit. All the lads cheer when I walk in.

Day four

Today we will go to Lord's and after rain delays the start of play until 3.45 p.m. we will lose our last five wickets for 22 runs. We will lose the first Test by 239 runs. We will be one-nil down in an Ashes series yet again, the sixth time out of the last eight in fact. It looks bad. It looks bad and it feels worse, but there's something different about it, something that hasn't happened before.

That first morning. That first day. We had them. We felt it, and they felt it too. It was a real fight, a real war. Then their big men stood up. Glenn McGrath at the Pavilion End. Shane Warne at the Nursery End. McGrath 5-53 and 4-29. Warne 2-19 and 4-64.

Clarke and Katich got runs, but Hayden didn't and Ponting didn't and Langer didn't and Gilchrist didn't.

Hoggy got Hayden again. Fred got Gilchrist twice. Patterns were beginning to form. Doubts were emerging and growing... Doubts and fears...

McGrath and Warne on top, the legends bailing them out, doing what the legends do, but we were in the game, and we were together. They knew it, and we knew it.

In the dressing room afterwards, I sit with Kev for a while. He's relieved and excited. Fifty-seven and 64 not out in his first Test match, fourteen fours and four sixes in all. He did what he said we should do at the team meeting in the Landmark. He smacked Shane Warne into the top tier of the Pavilion. He hit McGrath into the lower tier too. He hit Brett Lee into the Tavern. He played his shots and he pushed them back and he justified his selection, even with all of the pressure that was on him.

Michael Vaughan calls us together.

'Look lads, we start again at Edgbaston like it's nil-nil. It's a clean slate up there. You know we can beat this lot.'

It's exactly what we need to hear. Vaughan is brilliant at assessing the mood and saying the right thing. He's always calm, however nuts everything else is.

We pick up our kit, clear the dressing room, drift back to the Landmark. Matt Maynard, England's batting coach and a guy I've known since I was sixteen and joined the staff at Glamorgan, offers me a lift back to Wales.

I'm waiting for him outside, standing on the pavement talking to Steve Harmison. Three or four lads come over.

'Fucking lost again,' one says.

'You two are crap.'

It goes on like this for a few minutes. Harmi and I take it for a while. It's fair enough, they've paid their money. I try to talk to a couple of them, but they're not having it. Harmi's starting to tick. He's six feet five and from Ashington, and he knows how to handle himself. I'm twitching too. These guys won't leave it. Just then, Michael Vaughan comes out of the hotel.

'All right, lads,' he says to them, a big cheesy grin on his face, and with a couple of minutes of chat, everyone's laughing and joking and shaking hands. It's like magic. How does he do it?

'See you next week, boys,' he says to us, and smiles.

2. Pace

I am fifteen years old, in Zimbabwe on tour with Dyfed Schools, playing against a club side. The batsman is a thirty-year-old sheep farmer. He's not wearing a helmet. This is winding me up. My first ball is short and fast and hits him in the mouth. Blood everywhere. He spits three teeth out onto the pitch beside him and stares me down.

'Come on, then...' he says.

I run in again, bowl short again. I'm still wound up about the helmet, but I'm kind of worried by the tooth thing too. The guy is twice my size as well as twice my age. This one is even quicker, but he gets his head out of the way. He shakes his bat at me. The umpire pulls me aside and warns me to stop. I probably should do too, but that's not my nature...

I have always been fast. Fast bowler, fast runner, fast eater, did my schoolwork fast...that's how I got the nickname Horse – horses go fast, you see. The first time I realised that I could bowl quickly, I was twelve years old and playing for Llanelli Schools against a team from Worcester. This guy came in, a little bit bigger than the rest, and he started to bully the other bowlers. I thought, 'I'm not having that.' I gave him a short one, and it hit him on the forearm. I saw the tears on his face. I gave him another short one and it hit him on the forearm again, same place. Their coach came on and carried him off. I wasn't sure why they carried him because I'd hit him on the arm, but it turned out I'd broken it in two places.

I don't know where it came from, but it was always there. My twin brother Matthew and elder brother Richard could both bowl quickly, but not as quickly as me. My dad Jeff was fast too, in his day. He bowled left arm over for Glamorgan and England, with a perfect, cartwheeling action. He bowled a very famous, very fast spell against Leicestershire at Grace Road in 1965. He took five wickets before he conceded a run and finished with 8-11. He was said to be the quickest bowler in the County Championship that season, and the following winter he played for England against Australia. He was the leading wicket taker in those Ashes with fifteen. He got 6-118 at Adelaide, which was the best-ever by a Glamorgan bowler in the national side. The following winter he blocked out the final over of the final Test against West Indies in Georgetown to save the series, but that was to be his last cap. His career was finished at twenty-six – arthritis of the elbow.

He'd say to me, 'Si, you're ridiculously quick for your age,' and I knew that it was true because my dad understood what fast bowling was.

*

It's like having a superpower, it's a surge, an urge. It's a feeling like no other, to know that the opposition are worried about you, sometimes frightened of you physically and psychologically. I've had guys throwing up in the dressing-room toilets before facing me. I've had guys refusing to come in to bat.

I loved the buzz of it, the ritual. I had this ridiculously long run-up that I kept well into my first-class career. It was so long I could only bowl four or five overs before I'd be blowing out of my backside, but it was part of the theatre of it. Fast bowlers need to *look* fast. It's an attitude, a state of mind. I could be temperamental, a moody bugger, as Michael Vaughan used to call me. I had a short fuse. It all fitted together with the natural pace.

The pace came first though. Until I was seventeen or so, I was only five feet six, and skinny. I was quick then, always playing with lads a couple of years older, a couple of years bigger – my dad wanted me to get used to losing as well as winning. He wanted me to try all sports. I played football. I played rugby. Athletics. He knew I could be a cricketer, but he knew too that I had to want it for myself, not because he did.

I had a friend, who I won't name. We played cricket together a lot as we went up through the system. We turned pro at the same age. His dad pushed him. His dad never left him alone. He had a bowling machine at his house from when he was eleven or twelve.

He was a proper player, my mate, but I think he found it impossible to cope with failure because of the pressure he'd had throughout his life. He'd smash his kit if he was out for nought. I reckon it damaged him, and he was out of the game by the time he was twenty.

All my dad would say to me was: 'Boy, you're going to have more bad days than good, so you better get used to them.'

I was very lucky.

I went to Millfield School to play for Wales Under 15s and bowled very quickly. I knocked their kids over for not very many. They offered me a scholarship. Pace was already beginning to shape my life. The cricket coach at Millfield was the former England seamer Richard Ellison. Those years at school and with Wales are, when I look back now, a glorious, carefree haze of youth cricket, a time when the game represented nothing but pure fun.

Wales played against Dorset a lot. They called us the Sheepshaggers. They were a good side, a big county with a lot of players. We'd come up against one another year-on-year, lads like Tom Hands and Ryan Driver. I fractured Tom's eye socket in the U13s – back then youth cricketers weren't required to wear helmets. Perhaps they didn't think the bowlers were quick enough to need them. I was, and because I was short, the ball skidded rather than really bounced, so I hit a lot of people.

The English lads always seemed bigger and stronger, slightly ahead. Wales Under 15s played England Under 14s, a game in which Graeme Swann edged me for six fours in an over, all of them through third man. He was a brilliant, natural player even then, and just as full of himself. He wound me up beautifully, played me like a song, and my temper built with every ball he got his bat on. I bowled shorter and shorter, faster and faster, and each one went flying to the rope accompanied by that familiar grin.

'Bloody hell, mate, that was quick,' he said afterwards. 'Don't worry about the runs, just keep doing that.'

In my last year at school word began to spread. My dad had some contacts down in Essex, and so John Lever and Keith Fletcher came to Millfield to see me bowl. I'd been spending a lot of time in the gym and I'd had a few heavy sessions in the days before the trial so I was sore and didn't bowl particularly quickly. They weren't impressed. Glamorgan were the obvious choice for me, but my dad knew the set up there and was wary. They had a reputation of not coming in for players until other counties started buzzing around. As soon as they got wind of the Essex trial, Matthew Maynard, the club captain, came to Millfield to see me bowl too. This time I chilled for a few days, stayed out of the gym, and bowled like the wind in front of Matty. His eyes lit up. Glamorgan hadn't had a really quick Welsh lad since Greg Thomas. Within a week they'd offered me a contract.

Sixteen years old, still at school, a professional cricketer. I couldn't have been happier or more proud.

Because I was in my last year at Millfield I could only play for part of the summer. When I got to the Glamorgan dressing room, I barely spoke to these pro cricketers who to me were legends, heroes. I was shy and wordless, but with the ball in my hand I was wild. I just wanted to run in and let it go off my endless run-up. I had no radar at all – it could go anywhere. I bowled a beamer to Matt Maynard in the nets and hit him on the gloves. Bowling a beamer to the Glamorgan captain – I thought I might get a bat around the head.

Matty let it go. He could see that I was quick and getting quicker. If I could hit him, I could hit anyone. He liked the idea of that.

I had my growth spurt. I went from five feet six and skinny to six feet three and strong. I went from bowling mid-80s mph to 90-plus. During the summer that I was eighteen, Matt began using me as a twelfth man for the first team, so that I could start to get a feel for it. He knew I'd be there soon enough.

The Glamorgan changing room was actually two rooms, one for second-team players and one for the first team. When you went across from second to first, you knocked on the door and you spoke when you were spoken to. I could go for a couple of hours without saying anything at all. I wasn't sure where to sit, what to do. I was in awe of the guys in there: Matty Maynard, Robert Croft, Tony Cottee, Steve James, Adrian Dale, Waqar Younis. People I'd seen on TV. People whose names I read in the paper. My dad had brought me up to show respect, and I did.

I was soon recruited as Robert Croft's driver. It meant I had to go to the pub with him every night after the game and drive him home afterwards. I'd often find myself in one of Crofty's favoured boozers standing next to Devon Malcolm or Andy Caddick and soaking up every word they said. I learned so much just listening to them. At one of my first games I went to take a shower and the only other guy in there was Courtney Walsh. I stood there staring at him. Courtney Walsh! He probably thought I was some sort of weirdo, but he winked at me and wandered off.

I loved those days, loved being the tearaway young quick with no responsibility other than to run up and bowl fast. And I was brutally fast. I think that I was at my quickest before I was twenty.

I went to Pontypridd for a second-team game. Colin Metson, the first-team keeper, was playing. He'd kept to a lot of quick bowlers. He didn't know where to stand to me, so he went about fifteen yards back. The wicket had a bit of carry that day. Fifteen yards was nowhere near enough. I hit him hard; the first ball almost ripped him off his feet. He said afterwards I was the quickest he'd kept to since Wayne Daniel.

I couldn't believe the aggression that the pros showed. One of my early first-class games was up at Durham. It was a quick wicket there because they had a team full of fast bowlers. They knew that we played on a real pudding at Sophia Gardens so they wanted to knock us back a bit. I bowled to David Boon and John Morris. I'd only ever seen Boon on the television. I couldn't believe how good he was. Just rock solid.

I nicked him off early, but it got dropped. I was gutted by that. He would have been a huge wicket for me. Then he and Morris got stuck in. They called John 'Animal', and that day I discovered why. He'd had a run-in with some of the management at Durham. He was seriously fucked off and he took it out on us. He picked a fight with Steve James, who was probably the nicest man in cricket. He was swearing at us, at the crowd, everyone. He made a double hundred, and when he hit the boundary that got him there he was yelling and giving two fingers to the executives up in the offices. I thought that the umpires would step in – you know, 'Come on, lads, you're playing first-class cricket now.' But no. They just let it go, let us get on with it, and everyone got stuck in.

I revelled in it, bloody loved it. When I moved up to the first team, the rumours started going around not just that I was quick, but that I was nasty and wayward, too. The rumours were true. I just wanted to bowl as fast as I could, and Matty Maynard encouraged me. He'd stand at first slip, winding me up. He knew he'd get a reaction because that was my character. Quiet and respectful off the pitch. A proper handful on it.

There was some sort of fast-bowling contest going on that summer. A speed gun was going around the counties. Matthew Hoggard won with 86 mph – he was at his sharpest when he was younger too. Steve Watkin, our opening bowler, laughed at it. 'You're way quicker than that,' he said. 'I don't think there's anyone quicker on the circuit.'

That was a big incentive to me. I wanted to be known and feared. I was fearless. We went up to Blackpool to play against Lancashire. The wicket was slow and green but that didn't stop me. I went hard at Mike Atherton. He was a legend of the game. He'd faced down every quick bowler on the planet. Matty was riling me from first slip. Andrew Flintoff was batting at the other end. I flew in to Athers, and I hurried him a few times. I gave him a good short one that he spooned up in the air to mid-on where Darren Thomas dropped it. Gutted about that one, too.

I said to Flintoff: 'You better stay that end, Fred, 'cos you're shitting yourself.'

He still reminds me about that line.

41

But Atherton gave me absolutely nothing. I peppered him, tried to knock him over, swore at him, chirruped away…and he just stared at me. I learned how tough and hard the really top players could be.

That Lancashire game was the one where our physio heard a couple of guys throwing up before going out to face me. It couldn't last. It never does. I was this raw thing, a nerve-end in the wind. I had speed but no real skill. Sometimes the ball swung, sometimes it didn't. Sometimes I took wickets, sometimes I didn't.

This first, bright burst still lives in my head as the purest expression of the pace I had. I understood that it would begin to change. If I wanted a career in the game, I had to add some range to my voice.

But pace is one of cricket's most valuable currencies precisely because it is so rare. Those last few miles per hour between the mid-80s and the 90s are vital in stopping the very best batsmen, and few people on earth can produce them. Every mile per hour that can be pulled out above ninety is worth its weight. The difference between facing a ball delivered at 90 mph and 95 mph is only measured in the smallest fractions of seconds, but that gulf is vast. There's just no comparison in how it feels. I would discover, when I played Test cricket, that 90-plus mph took me to the limits of what I could actually see and then put a bat on. Once I'd faced 90-plus, mid-80s seemed like spin.

I was still growing, still filling out. My run-up was ridiculous and my action non-sustainable. I began to accrue injuries: a couple of stress fractures and a fascia disc problem. The stress fractures were due to some badly fitted insoles in my boots. The back problem was rooted in my action itself. I had a counter rotation: my bottom half was square on to the batsman when I landed in my delivery stride, but my top half was side-on. This resistance gave me some of my speed, but my back couldn't take the torque that it imparted. My natural action was to pull my bowling arm way back behind my right ear as I wound up, which added more rotation into the mix.

Duncan Fletcher was the first to speak to me about cutting down my run. A lot of my power has always come from my body action rather than the momentum from the run, and as I grew and became physically stronger I could bowl very quickly from just a few paces.

I skidded onto England's radar. I joined the initial Academy intake, where I met Rod Marsh and Troy Cooley for the first time. Rod cut my run down until it was very short. Troy remodelled my action, which took probably eighteen months to feel entirely natural. I worked on it in practice and then slowly introduced it to matches. It took time because as soon as I was put under pressure in a game, I'd revert to what I knew. This is entirely normal. I'd watch videos back and see it happening.

Duncan Fletcher argued with Rod Marsh about my run-up. Fletch wanted it longer again. Rod thought I was still just as quick from the very short version. Duncan won. By the time I made my international debut, I'd changed almost everything about my bowling: run-up, action, grip.

It was Troy who taught me how to reverse-swing the ball, this new and counter-intuitive skill that would begin to set me apart. I was stronger, fitter and properly equipped for the big time.

But I was never again as quick. I felt, deep down, that I was limiting myself. I knew that it was the right thing to do. It was the only thing to do. My body wouldn't have sustained bowling in the way I was. But fast bowlers want to bowl as fast as they can, and faster than anyone else. That was my nature, my need.

The raw, wild pace of youth…It was gone by the time I was twenty, but what a thing it was.

I'm still quick now, don't worry about that. Even after all of the injuries and pain. Even with the shell of a left knee, and all of the other aches and breaks. I play occasional games for the Professional Cricketers' Association, and I can bowl mid-80s from four or five paces. One player I'd have loved to have tested myself against is Steve Waugh. He was playing at Brisbane when I injured my knee. That was the only chance I had, and it ended before it began.

However, a little while ago I played a knockabout charity game in LA, and he was in the oppo team. I was messing about off a few paces when he came in. As soon as he did, I started banging it down three or four yards more quickly, couldn't stop myself. He'd not played for a while, but those eyes narrowed to slits as he realised what was happening. He could no more stop himself from digging in than I could from bowling as quickly as I could.

He looked down the wicket and smiled at me. For once, I smiled back.

3. Edgbaston

*In which I drink away the agony of defeat, witness the felling
of an Australian legend, feel the pain of bone on bone,
and temporarily drop the Ashes...*

W e're going back home to Wales from Lord's, Matt
Maynard at the wheel, me in the passenger's seat.
I don't like driving in London, and I don't suppose Matty
would be too happy if I was either because we've just stopped
and bought a twelve-pack of cans, and I'm working my way
through them pretty well as he guns it up the M4, out of town
and towards God's country.

'Bloody hell, Horse, don't hold back, will you.'

'I won't mate...I won't...'

By the time we get to Cardiff, the cans have gone.

The booze turns the next few days a little more soft-focus. I
mooch around the flat, watch TV, let Lord's and everything
about it ease out of my system. It doesn't take too long.

The nature of sport is that it's forward-looking. You have to be pragmatic or everything about it – the endless uncertainty, the constant what-ifs that arise from every game, every day – would eat away at you. It could become a long game of *Sliding Doors* in which you torture yourself with every road not taken.

The alcohol helps. Fletch doesn't mind us tying one on after a Test as long as there's recovery time before the next. Sometimes you need it.

What's gnawing away at me are not the missed opportunities at Lord's but the pain in my ankle. Fast bowling is about pain. I think if you asked any quick bowler how often they bowled completely pain-free it would be about 5 per cent of their career, probably at the very start before the daily grind of it begins to take the physique apart piece by piece. The human body simply isn't built to withstand the constant repetition of the run-up and bowling action.

Pain is why I start every day with a couple of ibuprofen and two paracetamol – 'the fast bowler's breakfast' as it's known. It's why Troy Cooley tells us not to go more than three or four days without bowling: any longer and you get DOMS – delayed onset muscle soreness – that really kills you. Pain is why I spend as much time with Kirk Russell, England's physio, as I do with my family.

I know the pain register well. I know the difference between everyday pain and something more serious. I know what I can play through today, and what will be a problem next week. The pain in my ankle isn't quotidian, the kind that you just soldier on with. It's higher on the pain register than that. I have a bone-spur caused by an old injury, and it is digging into the soft tissue around the front of my foot, sometimes coming into direct bone-on-bone contact with the joint above. Behind the ankle are a couple of smaller spurs.

We've decided that I'll have a cortisone jab to get me through the next couple of Tests. Cortisone is a powerful steroid that reduces inflammation. At the same time, they'll inject a local anaesthetic that will numb the whole ankle. It doesn't actually solve the problem, it just means you can't feel it for a while – two to three weeks at least. For that reason, you're not supposed to have more than three cortisone injections in your life. I've already had two.

I have the jab anyway. I'm desperate for it. I'd take whatever, just to play in some more of this series – one more game, two more games, three... It fucking hurts though. It's a long needle. Once it's done, I see Kirk every morning so that he can wrap cloth bands around my foot and hyperextend the joint by pulling hard on the bands, which makes it easier to get it moving. The local anaesthetic is odd, my foot feels as if it's there but it's not and for a while when I'm bowling in the nets it's hard to know exactly where it is on the crease. Yet it's a lot better than crashing the ankle down onto the hard ground time after time with nothing but a few ibuprofen to dull the pain. Within a couple of days, the cortisone kicks in.

The omens for the second Test are odd and unsettling. Three days before we arrive in Birmingham, a tornado blows through the city, uprooting a thousand trees, picking up cars and tearing off roofs. It passes within 400 yards of Edgbaston. The storm that follows in the tornado's wake dumps an inch of rain onto the pitch in around sixty seconds. The covers that are supposed to protect the wicket end up floating on top of it. No one, including the head groundsman Steve Rouse, knows what effect this will have, because nothing like it has ever happened before. The crust of the pitch is firm. The deeper ground is drenched. Steve's best guess is that the wicket will be slow, but he can't be sure – in terms of preparation it's about four days behind where it should be for the start of a game, and therefore unpredictable.

We get called into a meeting and told that there are rumours of a terrorist attack on the dressing rooms during the game. We're told that security has been tightened and that we are in no danger. It's another niggle though, another strange thing that adds to the natural uncertainties of the days before a big match. To combat it, we have the usual routines. We arrive on the Monday and have the team meeting; have a hard session on the Tuesday; train light on the Wednesday; play on the Thursday. These are the rhythms that reassure us, that keep things normal, controlled.

I know that Fletch and Troy and the coaching staff will be looking for any sign that my ankle's a problem. Through Tuesday's session I feel their eyes on me. I go hard, probably harder than I need to. I get right through the crease when I'm bowling; chase down my high balls in the field; show no sign of pain or weakness, even though I know it's there if I yield to it.

Our catching at Lord's was poor, so we work madly on it. I'm the designated thrower when Fletch drills the slip cordon. They fan out behind him while I chuck balls at him hard and he uses a bat to flick catches. He doesn't wear a glove, and if I whack him on the hand it'll make a mess of his knuckles, but he never misses. A couple get too close to his body and he drops his hand off the bat, catches them and gives me the stare.

We all know the stare, but there is a distance between him and the players that means we don't really know the man behind it. Fletch can be a disconcerting presence. The batters say that they can feel his eyes on them when he arrives soundlessly behind the nets to watch them. He often wears these reflector shades, which make him even more unreadable. He says very little. He hates lateness. He likes his batsmen to use the forward press and his quick bowlers to hit 90 mph. His instructions are simple and clear. If you don't remember them, or you don't execute properly – the stare. It's worse than a bollocking, and he understands the power of that. He'll change with us in the rooms, and he joins in the banter, but no one gives it back to him.

I knew him briefly at Glamorgan when I was a young kid and he was coach there, before he left to join England. I liked him, and he liked me, but there was still the distance. He used to wear these white socks. Robert Croft went into the dressing room at Sophia Gardens when Fletch wasn't there and he cut the feet out of them. We were all sitting around when Fletch came in to get changed. He stripped naked and went to put his socks on. He pulled the first one up and it just kept going. Crofty was trying not to laugh, but he was the only one. Fletch pulled the second sock up. By now some of the guys couldn't look. It was a super slo-mo car crash moment. Fletch didn't say anything. One by one, he pulled the other socks from his bag and looked at them. Silence. The stare...

Crofty never did that again.

Fletch didn't play Test cricket because Zimbabwe were an associate nation that only played limited-overs internationals. He was their all-rounder and captain, and led them to a famous win against Australia in the World Cup. He had the bloody-mindedness of the underdog, and because he had to maximise any small advantage in his team or weakness in his opponents', he developed an acute cricketing mind. His knowledge of technique seems endless, and he approaches it rigorously. He is logical and scientific, remorseless on drills, a disciple of repetition and practice, and yet his final instructions are always for us to express ourselves, to play naturally and without fear.

The drills though…Jeez, they're relentless, especially after Lord's. The Tuesday fielding session is without mercy. After the slipping, we have high catches – ten in a row, while having to sprint between each. Drop one and you start again at zero. Then ground fielding: two cones behind you, and you have to stop the ball going past you and through them, except the ball is absolutely fired at you from about twenty yards away.

I go hard, show no weakness. Fletch seems happy enough, behind the shades.

Day one

For some reason the sides warm up about thirty yards away from one another. Perhaps it's another John Buchanan thing – Sun Tzu, *The Art Of War* and all that stuff he likes to bang on about. At Lord's he'd made Australia train on the side of the ground that we normally used. We didn't care, we just moved over.

We have some catches and then a kick around with a football.

The Australians are playing touch rugby. At some point the laughs turn to shouts, there's some urgent movement, a huddle. Someone drives a golf buggy onto the field. The Australians are standing around a guy lying on the ground. I'm the closest England player to it.

'Have a look, Jonah…'

Glenn McGrath's on the floor, his right leg stretched out in front of him. He's sitting up but his face is bone white. His eyes are closed. As the physio pulls at the sock around his ankle, he covers his face with his forearm. My first thought is, 'There's no way he's playing in this game.'

I walk over and tell the lads.

'It's McGrath.'

We try and keep quiet, but an electric buzz passes around the group. They get McGrath onto the cart and drive him to the Pavilion.

Players aren't lying when they say that they want to play against the best, beat the best. We want to beat this Australian side because they're probably the greatest team in cricket history. But when something like this happens it's pointless to deny that it gives everyone a rush. However much of a chance we think we've got, the truth is, we're 1–0 down, and the man mostly responsible for that is now flat on his back on the physio's table.

We drift back to the Pavilion. The dressing rooms at Edgbaston are close together. The physio's rooms are between the two. Vaughany asks me to go in and find out what's going on. McGrath's lying down, still pale and obviously in pain. He trod on a ball that someone had left on the outfield where they were playing rugby. He turned the ankle right over. It can't take any weight at all. I hang around as long as I can, asking questions, but they start getting edgy and ask me to go.

I'm certain he won't play. If a fast bowler is showing that much pain, he's seriously hurting. We won't know for sure until the teams are exchanged at the toss, but McGrath's out.

Fletch and Vaughany have spent hours weighing up the pitch, speaking to Steve Rouse, looking at forecasts and conditions. We're sure that we want to bat. There's a chance that the wicket will behave unpredictably, but it's more likely to have been deadened by the rain. The only problem is that Michael never wins the toss, certainly not twice in a row. The toss is the worst part about the first day of a game. It takes place half an hour before the start of play, so from the moment I wake up, all I'm ever thinking is, 'Am I bowling today…am I bowling today…?'

I go to the massage room. Kirk hyperextends my ankle. *Am I bowling today…?*

There's no TV in here, but they've run some speakers through so that we can hear the broadcast. The captains go out.

Come on Vaughany for fuck's sake…you've got to win one soon…A day with my feet up would mean another day for the cortisone to settle my ankle. Another day stronger…

Mark Nicholas is MC-ing the toss for Channel Four, babbling on…

Get on with it…bloody well get on with it…

The coin goes up. Through the speakers I hear Mark Nicholas say, 'It's a head…Australia have won the toss.'

Balls…Again?

'Ricky, what are you going to do?'

'We're going to have a bowl, Mark.'

'WHAT...?'

I can't stop myself shouting. Holy fuck. McGrath's not playing – it's official now – and Punter's *bowling*?

Maybe he's misread the pitch.

Maybe he's sending a message to his team: 'You're good enough without him.'

Maybe he's sending a message to us: 'We'll beat you anyway.'

Whichever, I don't care. Vaughany gets back and he can't believe it either. The dressing room is buzzing.

No McGrath...Not here...Not today...

He has been replaced by Mike Kasprowicz. Kasper's a good mate of mine. We played together at Glamorgan. He's a strong bowler, good in English conditions. He's not Glenn McGrath though.

Maybe we've misread the pitch...Maybe they'll beat us anyway...

The Australians take the field. Trescothick and Strauss walk out behind them.

The tornado. The flood. The bomb scare. McGrath's ankle. The Edgbaston omens...

Packed house. The usual hush as ten-thirty ticks around. Brett Lee opens the bowling for Australia. Brett Lee runs in for the first ball. Right arm over the wicket. Tres on strike. Tres the leftie. Brett Lee fires it miles outside off stump, so far outside that Billy Bowden calls it a wide.

A wide first ball...

Brett Lee runs in again. This one is again wide outside the off stump, so wide it's an easy leave for Trescothick. The new ball bounces twice before it reaches Adam Gilchrist.

The lost toss... the dead wicket...

Jason Gillespie gets the other end. Strauss leaves the first three and hits the fourth ball for four through third man.

Brett Lee runs in for his second over. Trescothick check-drives his first ball to the cover boundary for four. Lee comes in again. Trescothick check-drives his fifth ball to the cover boundary for four. Lee comes in again. Trescothick hits his sixth ball to the cover boundary for four, but this time he doesn't bother checking the shot. He knows already how flat the pitch is and he swings hard and absolutely creams it, the ball smacking into the advertising board before Brett Lee's finished his follow through.

The omens of Edgbaston.... Good for us... Not for them...

Jason Gillespie bowls to Andrew Strauss, who nicks the third ball of his second over to first slip, where Shane Warne drops a hard chance low to his left.

Tres hits Lee for four more... Straussy hits Gillespie for four...

Gillespie bowls the eighth over of the innings. Tres whacks the first ball for four. Strauss hammers the fifth through point for another. Nine from that over. Six from the next.

After ten overs have been bowled we are 44-0.

Ponting takes Lee off and brings Kasprowicz on. Strauss hits his fifth ball for four. Gillespie gives everything he has to a short one and Tres seems to have all day to smack it to the fine leg boundary.

Shane Warne must come on to bowl the fourteenth over of the innings, when the ball is still new... Strauss walks down the wicket to his fourth delivery and hits it back over his head for four. The new ball gets soaked by the wet ground just beyond the boundary marker and the umpires call for drinks while a towel comes out to dry it. Drinks in the middle of an over...A soaking wet ball...Shane Warne on after an hour of the first morning...

The omens of Edgbaston...

A rumour goes around that Ponting and Warne have had a massive bust-up after Ponting came back in from the toss.

In Warne's next over, Strauss square drives for four and slog-sweeps another. In Warne's next, Tres hits him for a huge six back over his head. Then he creams Kasper for two more.

It goes on. The hundred comes up in the twenty-third over, when Strauss again strikes Kasprowicz for consecutive boundaries, and we're absolutely killing them here, murdering them.

Us and them at war...Ponting and Warne at war too...

Then, in the penultimate over before lunch, when Ponting needs it most, Warne throws one out wide to Straussy and, on the flat, dead Edgbaston pitch, it bites and turns and eludes his cut-shot to smash into the off stump.

Vaughan goes in and takes a single. Trescothick takes another.

One over left. Brett Lee to bowl it. Trescothick to survive it, to see us safely through to the break and no more damage done.

Except he doesn't just survive, because England are no longer a team that simply survives, that simply hopes. Brett Lee's first ball is short and wide and Tres guides it to the third-man fence for four. Brett Lee's second ball is even shorter and even wider and this time Tres smashes it high into the air and over the third-man fence for six. Brett Lee's fourth ball is full and wide and Tres hits it to the cover boundary. Brett Lee's sixth ball is full and wide and Tres smashes that through cover too, not even breaking stride as he starts walking after it to the Pavilion, ready for lunch with England on 132-1.

Trescothick 77 not out from eighty-nine deliveries with thirteen fours and two sixes . . . Shane Warne seven overs for 40. Brett Lee seven overs for 43. Glenn McGrath in the hospital, having scans. Australia in the field having won the toss.

The omens of Edgbaston.

Maybe it's at lunch on day one at Edgbaston that I begin to realise what kind of series this is. There have been no fallow sessions, few fallow *hours*. Each side wants to dominate the other. Neither will take a backward step – not voluntarily, anyway. Instead there's a kind of manic intensity to the cricket that gives it an edge, that makes it sharp and hard. It's difficult to look away, even for me, and usually I'll go and have a sleep when we're batting, get my ankle up and rest, but not here, not today. I watch every ball, we all do, as Michael Vaughan and Marcus Trescothick walk back out after lunch and resume the helter-skelter assault on Australia's bowling.

There's no holding back, not when Vaughan and Tres score another thirty from the next five overs, nor when Tres feathers an edge through to Gilchrist from the bowling of Kasprowicz to fall for 90, nor when Ian Bell hits his first ball for two, his second for four and then edges his third to Gilchrist to give Kasper his second wicket of the over, nor when Vaughan skies a pull-shot from a skiddy Gillespie bouncer to Brett Lee on the fine leg fence to go for 24 and leave us on 187-4, the day still careening along with no one really in control of its momentum.

No one is backing off, not with KP and Fred at the crease, the partnership that all of England has been waiting to see. Not only will they take on Australia, they'll take on each other.

They look huge and daunting. Kev's on this unstoppable run that started with his one-day hundreds in South Africa and carried on at Bristol and then Lord's. He's like a man who's spent months slogging up a mountain and is now charging down the other side. Fred has carried years of expectation too, imposed not by himself but by others – 'the new Botham', the latest of many. He didn't enjoy Lord's but he's leaving that behind.

Ditching the fear, ditching the doubt…

They get to a fifty partnership in fifty deliveries. Kev gets to 30 from 36 deliveries with five fours. Fred gets to 30 from 31 balls, with three fours and two sixes. Kev blinks first. He eases back and knocks singles, giving Fred the strike, offering him the stage. Fred hooks Lee for six and lofts Warne over long-off for another. Then he hits a big leg-break through cover for four more. He hooks Lee for another six, and hits him for two more boundaries through gully to bring up the hundred partnership.

Kev hits Warnie inside out over cover.

Suddenly it's tea. England 289-4 from 54 overs. Flintoff 68. Pietersen 40. Shane Warne's 17 overs have cost 89. Brett Lee's 11 overs have cost 72.

I'm not sure I've ever seen a day's play like this one. Flintoff goes to Gillespie from the third ball after tea. Geraint Jones is out for just a single a few overs later. Ashley Giles goes in and hits his second ball for four. He edges another to bring up the 300.

Ponting takes off Kasprowicz and Gillespie and brings back Lee and Warne. Kev flicks the switch. He hits three of Lee's first six deliveries through cover for four. He swats Warne through square leg for another.

Warne hits Gilo on the toe with a straight one and Billy Bowden raises his crooked finger and gives him out. Seven down. I get my pads on. The way this is going, I'll bat today.

Kev hits Lee for another huge six over square leg. Two balls later, he pulls one straight to Katich and goes for 71 from seventy-six balls.

Harmi goes in. He tries to hook Brett Lee and top edges him for six. The dressing room goes nuts. Edgbaston goes nuttier. Lee turns red (or redder). Harmi pulls the next one for four, and then runs down the wicket to Shane Warne and hits him straight for four more. He tries to sweep Warne then changes his mind and he's bowled for 17 from 11 balls.

I go in. I edge Warne past slip for two. Then he bowls me a full toss. I clog it through square leg for four. The crowd noise is ridiculous. I play and miss at the next two.

'Fuck off, Jonah...' Warne says.

In the middle of all this, Hoggy has made 8 from forty-one balls and he's defending like Geoffrey Boycott. He finally gets a drive away.

'Fuck me...' Warne says to no one in particular. I think about the argument, the bust-up he's had with Ponting.

Gillespie comes back on. He's down in the low 80s mph. A part of me feels for him. Another part of me doesn't, so I have a big wahoo at his first ball and it sails back over his head for six. I'll give Kev this – his bats are good.

I hit Gillespie over mid-off for a couple and the crowd goes mad – I only realise why when Hoggy points up at the scoreboard and I see that the 400 is up. Four hundred runs in a day. I push Gillespie for a single and Hoggy hits the last ball of the over for four through cover. Gillespie hasn't got the energy to swear at him. He takes his sweater and walks away.

Tail-end runs kill captains and they kill bowlers, but they don't quite kill Shane Warne. The great champion comes in again and does Hoggy with a slider that he tries to sweep and misses.

The innings is over – 356 minutes, 79.2 overs, 407 runs, 10 wickets.

Tornados and bomb scares. McGrath in the hospital. Ponting and Warne at war.

One long, wild, weird day, a day like no other.

There are eight overs of play remaining, eight overs in which we could tear into Australia, but that will have to wait because the drizzle and the light mean that there will be no more cricket today.

Tomorrow we will bowl. Tomorrow, anything could happen.

England 407 all out, Trescothick 90, Pietersen 71, Flintoff 68; Warne 4-116.

Day two
Kev's got this hairstyle that the papers have started calling 'The Dead Skunk'. It's a sort of spiky mullet with a blond streak right

through the middle. He's not what you'd call inconspicuous. We go out to eat most nights, or somewhere for a quiet beer, and people have started recognising him. Because he was born in South Africa to an English mother he's travelled a long road to the England team and it hasn't always been an easy route. He rowed with South Africa over the quota system introduced to address racial discrimination after apartheid. He played for Kwa-Zulu Natal against England in a warm-up game in Durban and walked into England's dressing room afterwards, sat down next to Nasser Hussain, who was captain at the time, and asked him if he knew of any clubs he could play for in England. He was an off-spinner who batted a bit back then. He ended up as the pro at Cannock. Clive Rice was the coach at Nottinghamshire and he heard about Kev and got him in. Suddenly he turned from a bowler into a batsman: he got a hundred on his debut and then got stacks of runs for Notts – four hundreds in a row the following season – and got onto the ECB performance programme. He scored another stack of runs in India, then fell out with Notts after the captain threw his gear off the balcony when he asked if he could leave.

He went to Hampshire, got called up to the full one-day side in Zimbabwe, scored runs, was called into the squad for the limited overs part of the South Africa tour last winter and made 454 runs in five innings even though the South African crowds went for him relentlessly.

Despite his heavy scoring there was lots of talk that he was just a one-day player, too unorthodox to be a Test match batsman, but when he shredded the Australian bowling at Bristol it just seemed impossible to not have him in the side. Some players

– a very few – just have this extra something…you *feel* it more than anything. When we were batting together at Lord's and Brett Lee was bowling at 90 mph I could just about pick the ball up to get a bat on it. You have 0.4 seconds before it's down your end, after all. Kev could see it, decide which shot to play and put it into the stands. Rod Marsh has been head coach at Loughborough for four years and was at the Australian Academy for a decade before that. He doesn't give out praise easily. He said that Kev and Ricky Ponting are the best two young batsmen he's ever seen go through the system.

It's extremely unusual, actually unique, for a batsman of Kev's class to have been playing as a bowler until he was nearly twenty. Maybe that's partly what makes him want to prove himself. The shots, the hairstyle, the swagger…they suggest that he's the Big Man with the big ego, but all of the swagger is attached to his batting. On the field he's confident and imposing but beyond it he's a lovely guy, covering up his shyness and insecurity. We're all like that to certain degrees. I breathe fire when I bowl. I'm reserved away from the game. The inner life is a long way removed from the persona on the cricket pitch.

The Aussies are going hard at him, trying to work him out. When you first come into international cricket you have the slender advantage of your opponents not knowing everything about your technique and your character. So the Australians prod and probe at KP. They talk about his hair. They sledge him, swear at him, bring the field up and try and get him to hit it over the top. He's got a sponsorship deal with this new energy drink Red Bull and he's put their sticker on the bottom of his bat. The Australians have noticed it and they're giving him plenty of abuse. He just laughs at them. Three innings: 57, 64 not out, 71. Five sixes and twenty-four fours.

You've got to push them back…'

Maybe this Test becomes great during the first overs of Australia's innings on a morning of low summer cloud and cool air, when Langer and Hayden run out in front of a huge and bullish crowd, Langer tight and angry, Hayden tight and focused, Steve Harmison waiting for them at one end, Matthew Hoggard waiting for them at the other, just like Lord's when we hit them hard with the new ball.

And it *is* just like Lord's when Steve Harmison runs in for his third ball of the day and smacks Langer square on the helmet. Langer's as tough as anyone in the game, but we can see he's shaken up. Who wouldn't be?

Hayden is at the other end, waiting for Matthew Hoggard. For years now he has been the enforcer at the top of Australia's order, the man who called his straight drive 'the bowler killer' because he hits it back so hard at them it may break their bones. But this summer has been fallow, this summer against England with white ball and red he has scores of 6, 31, 39, 14, 17, 17, 31, 12 and 34. He has not made a Test match hundred for twenty-four innings and counting.

Now he must face Matthew Hoggard, who clean bowled him at Lord's, and his first ball is full and tempting, nice and juicy, the kind of ball that Haydos has made a career from pounding to the boundary…except that late in its flight it's moving away, far enough away to catch the outside half of the bat and rocket at head height to Andrew Strauss at short cover, placed there for exactly this ball, exactly this shot, exactly this moment.

Hayden gone first ball and Edgbaston absolutely erupts with joy, a phenomenal noise that adds to *our* joy.

The next hour is proper Test match cricket, as hard and rough and tense as you like. It's an hour that begins with a panicky first-ball single from Ricky Ponting – Kev fields his defensive push and has a shy at the stumps with Ponting yards out if he hits.

But Punter rides it out. Although Harmi is finding bounce and pace in this wicket, Ponting and Langer fire back, Ponting playing a couple of pulls that crack from his bat, Langer hooking and fending and cutting, his eyes narrow, his mouth thin.

I get on for the ninth over of the innings and it comes out pretty well, no swing but my pace is good and so's my line and length. Early in the summer Troy Cooley and Fletch suggested that I change my grip a little, so now I split my index and middle fingers wider on either side of the seam and it offers me much more control with no less pace. Small margins are everything here. I bang out twelve good balls in a row to Ponting and he can't score, can't get me away, and I know that soon he'll be looking for a big shot because he doesn't like being kept quiet by any bowler, no matter where, no matter what the score.

He gets on strike to Harmison, who has changed ends, and suddenly there's another pull-shot and a clip through midwicket and the spell is broken. In my next over he hits me for three consecutive boundaries, one to long-off, one to long-on and the third through midwicket to bring up his fifty.

Vaughany hooks me off and puts Gilo on. I'm pissed off

and disappointed with myself. Ponting whacks Gilo for a couple more boundaries and all of a sudden he's got 60 and Australia are 87-1 from eighteen overs, scoring almost as freely as we did.

It's Gilo who turns it round. Gilo our forgotten hero. No one in the team takes more stick from the press than Ash, and we all know it; even though Fletch has banned papers from the dressing room, we still hear it, still read it. 'The Wheely Bin' they call him, which isn't much of name for a man who ripped out Brian Lara for his 100th Test match wicket, who has bowled England to wins over Pakistan and West Indies. Four years ago in India, to negate Tendulkar he'd bowled over the wicket, landing the ball outside leg stump and turning it towards Sachin's pads. Tendulkar kicked him away while the crowd in Bangalore worked itself into a fury with Gilo. Everyone remembered this and it affected the perceptions of his bowling, but what got forgotten was that Tendulkar had then lost his rag and charged down the wicket to be stumped.

Now, with five overs to go before lunch, Gilo goes over the wicket to Ricky Ponting and floats one down towards his pads, and Ponting plays an absolute nothing shot, a little dab-sweep that no one can recall him ever trying before, and the ball loops gently from the top edge to Vaughany, who's laughing before he's even taken the catch. He throws the ball up and charges towards Gilo, we all do, because this is Ashley's moment, on his home ground, dismissing the Australian captain, breaking the stand and blowing the innings open.

There is more magic to come, more magic with one ball to go before lunch, a ball that Damien Martyn pushes towards wide mid-on, and then he takes off and Vaughany chases around, picks up and throws, one stump to aim at, one stump that he hits on the bounce about halfway up – all those fielding drills from Fletch paying off. We gather round to watch the decision on the big screen, the bail lifting with Martyn six inches short of the crease.

I get the first crack after lunch but can't quite get it right. Anything short just sits in the pitch and anything slightly too full is being driven well by Clarke and Langer. I'm pushing a little too hard, wanting it just a little too much. Perhaps it's that, or perhaps there's just nothing in the wicket and nothing in the air, but I can't get it to swing, can't beat the bat, can't really even build any pressure, and after six overs I'm taken off.

Sometimes I still feel the scar of South Africa, when Vaughan didn't bowl me for two and a half sessions and I knew that I'd only get on when the ball started to reverse. I'm desperate to prove that I'm as good as anyone with the newer ball, and the frustration when it doesn't happen is almost overwhelming, but I have to keep my head on.

The fact that it's Clarke is eating at me. He's not quite a walking wicket for me but I knocked him over cheaply at Lord's twice – once in the NatWest final and also in the first innings of the Test, leg before both times. These are the battles that I want to win. I want to get into his head, make him dread having to start his innings against me, make it a theme that runs across the summer. He's regarded as the next great Australian batsman and perhaps he will be[1] but right now he's still the kid they call Pup, not quite as polished and tough as the players that come in above him. You can feel the difference. Men like Ponting, Langer, Hayden and Martyn have the rock solid quality that comes from match hardness. They've seen it all. They have self-knowledge. There are no secrets with guys like that. They know where they are weak and where they are strong. They know that we know it too. It's just a question of who executes best. Clarke lacks none of their ability but doesn't yet have their discipline or their judgement.

He's got himself in here though, on this slow, low wicket, and he and Langer start to eat into the deficit, repairing the pre-lunch damage. Langer is scoring more slowly than he usually would, but he's got that understanding of what's needed and he's subjugating his own desires for the requirements of the team. No loose shots. No chances taken. Patience shown, even when he's not feeling patient.

They take the score from 118 to 194. Vaughan is giving Gilo a good go and he's fighting hard. Both batsmen want to use their feet to get out to him, knock him off his length but he responds with great control and skill, and today is his day because just as Langer has got past fifty and Clarke is coming up to the milestone, right when Australia are about to bring up 200, he gets us the breakthrough again. Clarke

---

[1] After our duel throughout the 2005 series, Clarke would go on to take his place in the pantheon of great Australian batsmen, making more than 8,000 Test runs at an average of 50. As his country's 43rd captain, he defeated England 5–0 to regain the Ashes in 2013–14 and provided magnificent leadership during the dark days that followed the death of his friend and teammate Phillip Hughes.

has hit the first ball of his previous over for four in classical style, running down the wicket to drive the ball to the fence. Ash has him back on strike for the next. Perhaps Clarke is expecting Ash to throw the ball up again to show him that he won't back off, but Gilo's been taken on by big players before. He's knocked over Inzamam in Pakistan, Tendulkar in front of his own fans, Lara, Jayawardene. So often in Test cricket, this is what counts. Instead he pushes a fast, flat one across Clarke's stumps and Clarke dabs at it indecisively, edging it through to Geraint.

Boom – one end open again. Blood in the water. It's all we need.

Fred spears one across Katich, who nicks off.

Fred comes off, I come on. Right away it feels different. The rhythm is back. Gilchrist is in, so we've still got two left-handers to bowl at. I'm feeling good enough to go around the wicket to Gilchrist but stay over it to Langer. Second over, I've got some real heat going. Langer's on strike. I bowl him the perfect inswinging yorker that starts on off stump then decks back at him, makes him trip over his feet and lose balance, and then sinks deep into his pad bang in front of middle. Rudi Koertzen gives him the slow death and he's gone for 82.

Still no batsman has made a century in this series. Ponting and Langer have got in and passed fifty, and neither has gone on. That's rare, very rare. I think it shows how potent our bowling attack is, how relentless we can be. We hunt from both ends, no let up, no release. We back one another.

Gilo absolutely kippers Warne with a slower one that he misses by miles. I get Lee to hang his bat out and edge to second slip. Fred does Gillespie with a big inswinging yorker, and Kasper with an action replay next ball.

From 194-3 to 308 all out. We lead by 99.

Without McGrath and behind on first innings, it's Shane Warne who finds something to drag Australia back into the game, Shane Warne, the man who writes Australian history. When you see his hands, you understand how it is he does what he does. Warne is squat and broad-shouldered, not physically imposing but a man with aura, presence. His wrists are broad, the palms of his hands meaty. His fingers are maybe twice as thick as mine. The ring finger of his right hand, the one that he drags down the side of the ball, is even thicker than the rest. Although he is a slow bowler, there is tremendous power and physicality in what he does. He imparts huge amounts of energy into the ball as he bowls it, especially the one he sends down to Andrew Strauss with England's openers five deliveries away from the sanctuary of the dressing room.

With the score at 25-0 and no alarms, with the happy, boozy crowd singing football songs in drowsy end-of-play voices, Ponting has asked him to bowl the final over of the day. He opts to come around the wicket to Strauss and throws the first ball out into the rough left by the bowlers' footmarks. It turns far enough for Warne to shout immediately to his captain:

'Hey Punter...Punt...'

And the pair rearrange the field because Warne's antennae are up, the thick fingers are twitching, there's something here, something for him.

They bring up deep midwicket to stop the single and keep

Strauss on strike. Ponting moves from square leg to silly point. Damien Martyn comes in to a wide leg slip. Katich is at silly mid-on. Suddenly Strauss is surrounded on enemy land.

The next delivery is a huge side-spinner delivered from wide on the crease, a ball that pitches miles outside Strauss's off stump, that bites into the wicket and fizzes back at what looks like a right angle past Straussy's disbelieving, last-second attempt to kick it away, going past the off and middle stumps to somehow cannon into leg.

Jesus. It's one of those 'did that just happen' moments. Even Warne is laughing at his own audacity as his teammates mob him. They put the replay up on the big screen and the crowd gasps as they see how much the ball has deviated. Strauss stares at the pitch for a long time before he starts to walk off.[2]

Hoggard goes in as nightwatchman and survives the last four balls. It's the end of day two – just the 715 runs and 21 wickets so far. How does anyone follow that?

Australia 308, Langer 82, Ponting 61; Flintoff 3-52, Giles 3-78. England 25-1, lead by 124.

Day three
By rights, by any reasonable measure, day three at Edgbaston should be a dull one, or at least a *normal* one – a day of consolidation and cricketing sanity, but it's pretty obvious

---

[2] Straussy's wicket was Warne's 100th in England, the first time in history that any bowler had reached that mark in the home country of an opposing Test nation.

within a few overs of the resumption that it won't be, that it can't be, that this strange internal momentum that has gripped the match cannot be halted. Instead it clatters along like a runaway train, barely clinging to the rails.

In the calm of the dressing room, the plan we discuss is a simple one. Just bat. There are oceans of time left in this game. If we stay in for another four sessions we'll have an insurmountable lead and about 150 overs to bowl Australia out for a second time with the pressure of the scoreboard and the wearing pitch bearing down on them. It's just the kind of day a fast bowler loves – feet up, more rest for my ankle, which is feeling good (well, good in the sense of not yet catastrophically bad). As my mind drifts down this happy avenue, there's a hideous noise right in my ear:

'BAAAAAAA...'

It's Hoggard. He's been doing it all summer, waiting for me to zone out and then sneaking up to bleat like a sheep. Either that or bleating like a sheep into my voicemail until it runs out of memory. I'd forgotten he was nightwatchman – he's in first thing this morning and so he's restless and hyper.

'BAAAAAA...'

'Fuck off, Hoggy.'

He walks away laughing.

One hundred and twenty four behind having put us in to bat, McGrath injured and Warnie peeved, Ponting knows he has to go for it. He's as tough and stubborn as they come. He'll never admit that he got it wrong at the toss, and he'll believe absolutely that Australia will win this Test. They've been beating England for years and years. Why should this be any different?

He has to go for it and he does: Lee opens at one end, Warne at the other. Suddenly the crazy train is off the rails again. With the third ball of his second over, Lee induces a Trescothick edge. With the fifth ball of his second over he clean bowls Michael Vaughan. With the fifth ball of his third over he forces Hoggy to fend to Hayden in the gully.

From nowhere, we are 31-4.

Blood in the water again, but this time it's ours.

Lee is bowling beautifully. If you were to construct a fast bowler from the contents of the coaching manual, they would have Lee's long straight run, his athletic sprint that quickly and rhythmically gathers pace before transferring all of its energy through the final, gathering leap and into the braced front leg, the ball arrowing to its target from a perfectly cocked wrist. There are many ways to get the ball down the other end at 90-plus mph – just look at Harmi, me and Fred for example – but few are better to watch.

Except when you're facing him, of course, although the purity of his action does offer the earliest possible sight of the ball. That's small consolation to the three he has just dismissed, or to Kev and Ian Bell, who need to weather this storm and at least stop the clatter becoming a collapse.

Warne bowls a lovely over to Bell, who keeps it out.

Lee bowls a rapid over to Kev, who is hit on the shoulder. He takes a quick single to get on strike to Warne. He slog-sweeps his second ball from outside off stump into the stands. Warne stares at him and bowls a couple at his pads, which Kev blocks. Warne bowls another outside off. Kev hits him over long-on for another six. The score edges up...44 ...47...57...63...64...

Ponting needs something soon, and he gets it from Shane Warne, he gets it when Kev tries to sweep a ball that bounces a little more than he expects and it flies up around his pads, arm, bat, glove, and somehow Gilchrist sees it reappear and dives to grab it half an inch from the ground. Rudi Koertzen raises that slow finger, even though no one seems sure what part of Kev's body the ball actually hit.

He walks off, his eyes on the big screen.

Warne stays around the wicket to Bell for his next over and spins one right across his pads and onto the edge of the bat. More slow death...75-6.

Bloody hell, it's not even lunch yet. So much for four sessions.

There's still time for more pain, more worry when Fred goes back to a shorter delivery from Warne and falls down holding his left shoulder as soon as he's hit the ball. Kirk Russell is out there right away, and it doesn't look great. Fred's a big, strong man, used to physical pain on the cricket field, but his face betrays his angst. Kirk straightens him out and he stays on, hoping he can get through to lunch and have some proper treatment then. He makes it, just, after Gillespie gives him a short one that he paddles awkwardly down to fine leg.

Fred elects to bat on after lunch, but there's no respite for us, not with Brett Lee steaming in. In the first over after the break he gets Geraint with a throat ball that he can only fend to Ponting. Fred goes a bit do or die, flashing Lee to the third-man fence and then inside-edging him for four more. Lee gives him a mouthful. Fred belts Kasper for four. Gilo hangs in, soaking up deliveries when he has to. They add twenty. The lead edges towards 200. I reckon we can defend 230 if we have to. They add ten more before Warne gets Gilo with a big side-spinner that he nicks to slip. I get my pads on. Harmi goes out. Before I can get back to my seat, I hear the roar. Warne has done Steve first ball... 131-9.

The lead is 230. Shane Warne is on an Ashes hat-trick.

I walk down the steps, through the doors and onto the ground to face up.

He says nothing, just stares at me impassively. It's like Custer's last stand out here – everywhere I look there's an Australian face about two inches from mine. Gilly gees Warnie up, like he needs it. He makes me wait a long time, then he comes in, one step, two... and bowls a bloody awful one about three feet wide of off stump. I let it go. The crowd jeers or cheers – it's impossible to tell, it's just noise. He bowls again, another wide one and I take a swing. It flies through the close fielders for four.

Warne stares. Fred walks down the wicket laughing.

'Bloody hell, Horse, good shot, lad.'

We bump gloves. The fact that Freddie's relaxed relaxes me. He looks as if he hasn't a care in the world. Maybe he hasn't.

Kasper is on at the other end. Fred has a mighty wahoo at his first one and misses. The second is a no-ball that he smashes over midwicket and into the stands. I don't think he even heard the call, and it wouldn't have made much difference if he had – that ball was disappearing, legal or not. He cracks the next to mid-off hard, no run. Then he walks across his stumps and creams it absolutely miles into the air and beyond the rope. It disappears into the crowd and they swallow it with a roar. The sound of the ball leaving his bat is quite something. To Kasper he must look ten feet tall and ten feet wide. He charges at the next and slashes it out to the off-side sweeper for a single to leave me on strike.

I know that Kasper's going to try to nick me off so I'm ready for something outside off stump, and I mow it for four more. I smile at him. He stares at the sky, head thrown back in exasperation.

We have drinks. Fred doesn't care who's bowling now, doesn't give a shit about his shoulder or the state of the game. He's finally playing in an Ashes series, he's bowling like a demon and batting like a god and one is feeding the other. He's totally in the moment, and the moment is his. The crowd love it, love him; they inhale his ordinary greatness. It's like being on stage with Elvis out here.

Ponting takes off Kasper and goes back to Lee. Lee steams in but I'm seeing them okay and when I get some bat on a ball coming with his kind of heat it flies up over the field and away for four. Fred taps my glove.

He's on strike for Lee's next over. Lee is ticking now and he hurtles to the crease. I hear the grunt of effort as he lets the ball go. It's spearing in at the stumps, but Fred simply sits back in the crease and levers it up and over with a great whooshing swing of the bat. This one doesn't just land in the crowd, it goes

74

over the stand and out of the ground. I've never seen a cricket ball hit that far in my life.

'That were all right, weren't it, Jonah…'

They finally find the ball. Lee comes in again and Fred cuts him hard behind point. Clarke dives but he can't stop it. Billy Bowden's arm is out – another no-ball. Jeez – the wheels are coming off for Australia here. I look at Ponting. He's chewing hard. He's got everyone on the boundary, all of his plots and plans forgotten. Lee charges up and Fred pings the next one over long-on again. It really is pandemonium now, and I'm as caught up in it as everyone else. Flintoff is becoming a national hero right here in front of me.

I have a complete brain-fade to the next ball I face and don't play a shot to one that looks as if it's going to knock middle somewhere into next week. The Australians roar a huge appeal, but amazingly Billy doesn't give it.

It's a ridiculous bit of luck, but, although it makes the Aussies chunter, it doesn't make a lot of difference (or so we think), because a couple of overs and a few singles later, Freddie has another great wahoo at Warne and is bowled for 73. We have put on 51 runs for the last wicket, of which I have scored 12. As we arrive back in a buzzing dressing room, we all think that we have enough – 182 all out, and Australia need 282 to win.

So much for batting four sessions, then…

It's probably an even game, or at least a game that both sides believe that they can prevail, but we know that Fred has turned it back our way, we *feel* it, even though Warne is a genius and bowled like one,[3] even though Australians back themselves in any situation, especially against England. They are feeling our strength, our will not to be beaten; not here, not today. In the dressing room, Fred has the boombox and on goes 'Rocket Man' by Elton John. It's his theme song for the summer. We seem to hear it before every session: 'I'm a rocket man ...' over and over ...

Here come Langer and Hayden, Hayden on a king pair.

Harmi bowls a maiden to Langer.

Hoggy tries to get Hayden with the inswinger first ball, but it starts too straight and Hayden watches it pass down the leg side.

Hoggy looks for some swing but there is none. Hayden's big bat swishes through the line and gets one away to the boundary.

Langer, the small, angry man, is bristling. He hits Hoggy away for consecutive boundaries.

Despite the cloud cover and the deep red Duke's ball, there's no swing, no deviation for Hoggard, so Vaughan follows his intuition and throws it to Gilo in just the seventh over of the innings. Hayden comes down the pitch and murders one for four. A couple of overs later, Langer does the same.

Harmison is bowling quickly at the other end, but Hayden and Langer are playing him well, playing him easily. The score is 47-0, the target down to 242 with no problems, no alarms, no fear and no doubt.

---

[3] Warne's six dismissals in our second innings gave him ten for the match, and took his overall number of Test scalps to 599. He was in uncharted territory – no one in the history of the game had yet reached 600 wickets. Stranded one short, he would have to wait until Old Trafford to try again.

Vaughan gives me and Fred the signal to get warmed up. I can't wait to get back into them, to knock over Hayden, to knock over Langer, but first it's Flintoff. We gee him up because he's on a hat-trick after taking wickets with his final two deliveries of the first innings.

We make sure Langer knows it's a hat-trick ball too... anything to get into his head, change his mindset.

He ignores us and dances on the balls of his feet like a boxer.

Fred comes in around the wicket but he looks a little stiff, a little sore in the shoulder. He hits a length but Langer pushes it out easily into the off side. The crowd boo good-naturedly but it seems to lift them and lift Flintoff too. Maybe the adrenaline is kicking against the pain, but there's more zip as he comes in and bowls pretty much the same ball again, drawing Langer forward but this time it hits the seam and bounces, and instead of taking the middle of Langer's bat it smacks into the glove of his bottom hand and deflects down onto the off stump.

Now the crowd is up...now the spell is broken...now we're surrounding Fred and rubbing his head but he doesn't celebrate for long, he wastes no time in leaving us and walking back to the end of his run, letting Billy Bowden know that he'll be coming over the wicket now that he has Ricky Ponting on strike.

We've got an end open now, a new man in...the big man...the big wicket of the Australian captain.

The crowd roar as Flintoff runs in, a great throaty sound that gets louder the nearer he gets to the crease...

The ball is a huge in-ducker that scythes back at Ponting as he moves across his stumps, that smacks into his right pad just above the knee-roll, and the crowd are appealing before Fred is out of his follow through, before the slip cordon are up and screaming at Billy, before Fred turns to face Bowden himself and leaps high in the air, both arms outstretched.

Twenty-five thousand people, players and fans, all imploring Billy Bowden to raise his crooked finger and dismiss the captain of Australia, send him back to the pavilion for a first-ball duck, but Billy just shakes his head and says 'No' very gently.

The crowd boo. The slips let Ponting know how close it was. Flintoff puts his hands on his knees and blows out his cheeks. Ponting isolates himself in the middle of the pitch, flicking non-existent dirt from the wicket.

Flintoff comes in again, really hard this time, and bowls another heavy, back of a length delivery that has Ponting starting to square up as he goes across the stumps to cover any inswing. He edges it nervily down into the gully.

I see what Fred is doing here, and it's brilliant. Ponting knows Fred's got an outswinger and knows it's coming, but he has now faced two big inswingers that have dragged him in front of the stumps, where he doesn't want to be. His lips move as he watches Flintoff come in again.

Jesus, Fred must look huge as he charges towards you…

Ponting is waiting for that outswinger, waiting for it, ready, but Flintoff goes with the inswinger again, this one the biggest of the lot, and it goes late and fast past Ponting's bat and crashes into his front pad.

We're all up again, slips, crowd, Freddie, pleading with Billy Bowden, begging him to raise his finger, because this is the moment, this is the time that the match and the series go our way, not Australia's.

After eighteen years...

Billy shakes his head again, this time with more certainty than the last.

One more ball in this over. Surely this time it's the away swinger and it is, but Fred starts it too wide and although Ponting jumps nervily across the stumps, he lifts his bat and lets it through to Geraint.

But Billy Bowden's arm is out – no-ball.

Flintoff has one more crack. This time he absolutely nails it: the ball is seriously rapid and on a perfect line just outside off stump, a line that Ponting must play – but even as he does, even as he gets his back foot across, even as he brings down his bat, the ball is hitting the seam and spitting up and away from him, just far enough to take the edge as it continues to rise.

Geraint catches it in front of his face, and it's lucky he does because it would have taken all of his teeth out, so quickly is it still travelling.

Delirium. Fred is standing in the middle of the pitch, back arched, arms out, his head nodding up and down in acknowledgement of what he's just done. Vaughany jumps on him, we all surround him.

Ponting walks off, alone, the Edgbaston omens all around him.

Australia could crack here, plenty of sides would under the pressure and with the momentum that Flintoff has built, but

Australia don't. We work away at them. For eleven overs, nothing happens. The ankle is okay but I don't really like the end I'm bowling at. My temper builds, mostly at Matty Hayden. Off the field he's a decent bloke, but no one gives us more shit out there than big Buzz Lightyear. He's the classic tough-guy Aussie. He wants to bully us, with the bat and verbally. I let it wind me up a bit. Maybe I'm displacing the angst about my ankle; maybe I'm allowing Haydos and the fact I'd prefer to bowl at the other end get to me. Maybe I'm just being a moody bugger – it's not unknown.

Vaughany waits for a few overs and then he spells me and gets me on at the right end. Hayden on strike. The field's in a holding pattern: Tres at a wide first slip, Kev in the gully, the rest spread. First ball I go short and at the body and he pulls it for four. I try to make eye contact with him, but he's not having it. I rein in the ego, use my brain and go full. He drives the next two balls hard but straight to fielders. I go full again and he drives hard back past me for four.

They now need 200 to win with eight wickets in hand.

I run up hard and push one across him. He slaps his foot down the track and goes for another drive, but the ball just darts a little and he edges it high and hard towards the empty slip cordon. Out of nowhere, here comes Tres, flying like Batman to his left and grabbing it from the air.

'YES!'

Only that isn't quite what I say. I sprint down the pitch pointing towards the Pavilion, and give Haydos a good Welsh mouthful too. I might have called him 'Buzz...' Rudi Koertzen hears it, but I don't really care.

Hayden gone again in the thirties, the doubt and the fear still there, still growing. Two hundred still needed, but only seven wickets now.

And this time, finally, they do crack. Martyn clips Hoggard to Ian Bell at midwicket. Gilo has Katich caught at slip. Then he lures Gilchrist down the pitch to duff one to mid-on. Flintoff does Gillespie with another giant inswinging yorker: 137-7.

Warne starts swinging. He puts Ashley into the stands twice in a row. He's an awkward batsman to bowl to. He has a short backlift and he hits into unexpected areas. The sixes off Gilo are little more than short-arm prods. He nods at Michael Clarke, gees him up. Warne and Clarke are big mates. Kev and I see them out together all the time. Clarke plays and misses at Flintoff and Fred gives him a mouthful. Clarke gives him some back. Harmison comes on for Giles. With two overs left, Warne drives Fred for four. Fred almost yorks him in response.

Harmi bowls the last over. Clarke plays and misses at his first delivery. Harmi gives him two short ones, the first of which he almost fends to gully. He charges in again. This time it's a perfectly disguised slower delivery that Clarke plays all around, the ball thudding into the base of middle stump. Harmi jumps about twenty feet in the air. That's it, done. The last recognised batsman out to the last delivery of the day. For the first time anyone in this team can remember, Australia look beaten.

Clarke troops off, Warne behind him. Eight down, and 107 still required. Or curtains, as it's otherwise known.

England 407 and 182, Flintoff 71; Warne 6-46, Lee 4-82. Australia 308 and 175-8, Flintoff 3-34. Australia trail by 106.

Day four

We prepare as we usually do, no change in the routine, nothing different, nothing to suggest that today will be anything other than straightforward. We utter the usual clichés about taking nothing for granted, about sticking together and taking our chances and making sure that we relax and do exactly what we've been doing since this extraordinary match began.

But whatever anyone tells you, and whatever you tell yourself, it's just not possible. Beneath the surface calm I'm excited, happy, nervous, ready to get out there and finish Australia off, to beat them in a 'live' Test and square the Ashes series at one match all, having played as we know we can.

I'm not expecting to bowl. Vaughan has said he's starting with Harmison and Flintoff. It's their sort of wicket, and they have bowled best on it. I know that the skipper is thinking what we're all thinking: that Warnie will swing at a few; that Fred and Harmi will bowl a couple of deliveries that are good enough and we'll be back in here with our feet up in half an hour's time.

The crowd don't think that though, or if they do they don't care, because Edgbaston is full. Every seat taken for a game that might be over in five minutes.

Perhaps it's when Warne and Lee take thirteen runs from the fourth over of the day, and then eight from the fifth and nine from the sixth that I feel the first little tremor. Without doing very much they need another 66 to win.

I'm at third man on the Pavilion side and there's a group of Australian fans right behind me, giving me heaps.

'We'll only need fifty soon, Jones, you fucking plastic pom...'

Then Fred does it again, right when we need it, right when we need him. He swings one back in at Warne, who goes to flick it down the leg side but steps back too far and somehow kicks the bails off with his back foot.

He makes a loud 'OOOH' of shock and horror.

I turn around to the Australians and give them the fist-pump. They go nuts at me.

That must be it now, one wicket away and still 62 to get, Lee and Kasprowicz the last men at the crease.

Kasper knows one end of a bat from the other though, and somehow he keeps out a couple of brutal yorkers. Lee squeezes Fred through gully for four. Kasper edges one to fine leg for another.

Vaughan keeps Ash on. Lee and Kasper talk mid-pitch.

I'm saying to myself over and over, 'Be ready...be ready... this one's coming to you.' All of the Fletcher fielding drills are for moments like these, and you have to want the ball to come to you.

They decide to attack Gilo. It's the obvious move. There's no point blocking because sooner or later Fred or Harmi will bowl them something unplayable. All they can do is try to transfer the pressure back onto us – the pressure of getting over that line in front of your own fans, when there are no excuses not to.

Lee charges Gilo's first ball and carts it to cow corner for four. He takes a single. Kasper wafts the next over mid-off for four. He edges the next past slip for four more. I look up at the big electronic scoreboard. It says 'Runs to win 33'.

The Australians behind me are still chirruping.

'Christ, I didn't think even England could lose from here…'

Three runs come from the next Flintoff over. We have drinks. No one says much.

Gilo concedes three from his next over. Vaughan takes Flintoff off and brings Harmison on. Lee flicks a single. Kasper gets two through square leg. Harmi pushes a little too hard and sprays one wide of leg stump. It hits the footmarks and careens past Jonah for four byes.

I look at the big scoreboard. It says, 'Runs to win 20'.

Vaughan brings Flintoff on in place of Giles. Fred pounds one into the wicket and smacks Brett Lee on the hand. The physio comes on. Lee continues. Nothing on earth would force him off here. He takes a single. Harmi comes in. Lee Chinese cuts him back past his stumps for four.

Jesus. We're not actually going to lose this, are we?

I look at the big scoreboard. It says 'Runs to win 15'.

No, no, we'll get a chance. There's always a chance. It only takes one ball. And in a strange way, the pressure is on them now too. Both sides so near, so far.

I'm back at third man in front of the Aussie fans.

'How do you feel now, Jones, you fucking pom…'

I shut them out. There will be a chance. There always is. Fred bowls to Kasper. It's short of a length and lifting quickly. Kasper leans back and flips it up over the slips, high in the air and…

…straight towards me. I see it early, a dot against the clear blue sky. It's dropping short and slightly to my right, but this is it, this is the chance. I've caught hundreds of these, maybe thousands…

But then, as it drops below the skyline, the dark red ball disappears into the background of the big stand on the opposite side of the ground. When I see it again it's almost on the turf three or four feet in front of me. I fling myself forwards, too far forwards, and the ball smacks into my wrists and bounces away.

In that fraction of a second I understand that I've just lost us the match, and in all probability the series.

I jump up and fire the throw back in, but that doesn't matter, it's too little, too late. Fred has his hands on his head. The other lads are already back in position, not looking at me. I want to throw up. It is the worst feeling I've had on a cricket field. The England fans behind me are desolate. The Australians are dancing up and down and gesturing at me.

'Cheers, Jones... that was fucking useless, mate...'

I try to get my head back into the game, but I can't. All I can think about is the disappearing ball, but that's just an excuse... just an excuse because I've just dropped this fucking game...

Fred must be spewing because he steams in again and oversteps, the call of 'no-ball' still ringing out as the delivery spears down the leg side, swerving wide of Jonah's dive and rattling to the boundary to give them five runs.

Five runs. They need ten.

It seems no more than a few minutes ago we were a hundred ahead.

They get three singles.

Then another.

Then another.

Harmison and Flintoff are bowling their hearts out. Lee is battered and bruised but he's still there.

The big electric scoreboard says 'Runs to win 4'.

Harmi starts a new over to Lee. I'm out on the fence at deep cover. Vaughan goes to call me up into the ring but then decides no. Why let them win it with one hit?

I stay out, and Harmi's first ball is a wide, low full toss that Brett Lee absolutely creams right at me. I'm still thinking about the catch, about how it's lost us this game, so I don't notice quite how hard he's struck it, don't even bother going down on one knee for the long barrier, I just pick it up and chuck it back as hard as I can, hard enough to stop them coming back for two, hard enough to keep Kasper on strike.

The big electric scoreboard says 'Runs to win 3'.

How has this happened? Edgbaston omens?

Harmi to Kasper – rapid and on the stumps, Kasper pushes it back.

One loose ball now…one edge…one more piece of bad luck and we're done here…

Harmi to Kasper again. This time it's short and brutally quick – I don't know how Steve is keeping his pace this high – and because I'm perfectly side-on to the wicket I see in those tiny fractions of seconds that Kasper's in trouble here, because he's right across his stumps and he's actually ducking into the ball. As it rears up at his shoulder he flicks the bat instinctively and it hits his gloves and flies high and backwards towards Geraint who rolls to his left and comes up waving the ball above his head.

And then Billy Bowden is nodding *his* head and raising that lovely crooked finger, raising that glorious crooked finger up into the sky, and in the instant that he does, all of the dread and the sickness disappear, they disappear as if by magic to be replaced by a feeling of overwhelming joy that almost everyone in the ground is sharing. The next few minutes are bedlam, pandemonium, whatever other noun you can come up with.

I see Vaughany jumping on Fred and pulling his ears. I pile into the group that's hugging Geraint. He deserves this moment as much as anyone, because the Australians have targeted him all game, given him crap about his keeping, started calling him 'speedbump' because they reckon he doesn't stop anything, he just slows it down.

Well he just slowed you down, boys.

Later I will see the pictures of Freddie comforting Brett Lee, who is down on his haunches in despair, and I will admire him even more, because these are the moments in which we're human and imperfect and victorious.[4]

An hour later, when the crowd has gone and the ground is quiet and the joy has turned to relief and then into a kind of flat, bone-deep tiredness, I sit in the dressing room, holding an unopened beer that someone has shoved in my hand, trying to make sense of what just happened. Everyone is the same. It's as

---

[4] Our winning margin of two runs remains second on the list of the narrowest victories in Test cricket. Of the 2,156 Test matches played up until March 2015, only the West Indies' one-run win over Australia at Adelaide in 1993 has been closer. Coincidentally, the final wicket there also involved Australia's number 11, Craig McDermott, gloving a lifting ball to the wicketkeeper to end the match. Justin Langer and Shane Warne played in both games.

if we've caught a huge wave that has given us an exhilarating ride but has now dashed us on the stones of the beach.

There's a knock on the door. The Australians come in. The tradition in cricket is that the losers go to the winners' rooms, so we'd done the same at Lord's, but something has changed in the few days since then. We'd felt slightly sheepish at Lord's, because after all of the hype they had won quite easily. Here it is different. Here Australia are not quite sheepish, but they are not bullish either. They are as drained as we are. It feels as though we have gained their respect.

In the quiet rooms, on the empty ground, we drink together and talk about this astonishing game.

Four days later there's a DVD in the shops called *The Greatest Test Ever*.

4. Life In The Bubble

'*There you go Sheepshagger...*'

25 July, 2002. England versus India, first Test, Lord's. With these words England's captain Nasser Hussain hands me my brand-new cap. The lads in the circle around us clap and cheer. I pull it onto my head for the first time. I am about to become the 610th man to represent my country.

The presentation of the cap is a meaningful and significant moment, but Nasser knows exactly what to say, exactly how to say it. He's not just acknowledging (in a roundabout way) my Welshness, but finding the right words to put me at my ease and make me a part of the group.

It's a big moment, a big day, my biggest match.

Later, when I'm about to bowl for the first time, I say to him, 'Mate, I can't feel my legs.'

He laughs. Cheers, Nas.

'Don't worry. Enjoy it. You'll be all right. Trust what you've done with Troy. Pull that arm up and let it go...'

I still can't feel my legs, but I turn around and run in anyway.

In October 2001, the England and Wales Cricket Board decided to reinvent the way that cricketers were produced for the national side. For more than a decade, while England struggled, Australia had player after player coming into their Test and ODI teams, each apparently better than the last. The transitions between generations were seamless, their success uninterrupted. They could have fielded another eleven that would beat most other countries. At the heart of this success was their academy system and at the heart of the academy was Rod Marsh, an old-school Australian legend who had kept wicket to Lillee and Thomson and who knew exactly what it took to make it to the top of the game. Now the ECB had persuaded Marsh to come and work for them. They had set him up in Adelaide, and they were about to send him their first intake of players. On the initial list were Andrew Flintoff, Graeme Swann, Andrew Strauss, Rob Key, Ian Bell, Owais Shah, Chris Tremlett, Mark Wagh, Chris Schofield, Mark Wallace, Steve Kirby, Nicky Peng, Derek Kenway, Matthew Wood, Mark Wallace and Alex Tudor.

Steve Harmison and I, who were at the time considered the two quickest young bowlers in the country, were not included at first. They knew that Harmi struggled with being away from home for long periods. They felt I wasn't quite ready. Then they changed their minds.

A winter in the sun and a fee of £15,000 – I didn't need much persuading.

*

It was the hardest six months of my life, and it changed me radically. Before we flew they sent us to Sandhurst for six days to do some military training. We did the press-up test, the sit-up test, the two-mile run test where we were chased by a Land Rover that picked up anyone that fell off the pace. We were followed everywhere by these SAS guys. It was at night that the fun really started. We slept out in the woods in one-man tents. Flintoff doesn't like the dark, never has, and Harmison and Rob Key knew exactly how to terrify him. They'd sit and tell him ghost stories until he was too afraid to lie in his sleeping bag without his torch on. We'd just got off to sleep one night when an SAS guy accidentally banged against one of the guide ropes on Steve Kirby's tent.[1]

'OOS THAT? YOU'RE IN TROOBLE NAH…I'LL STAB YER…'

'Kirbs, he's a trained killer…'

'Oh, all right then…'

I loved it. They woke us up at 3 a.m. to tell us that they'd parked a Land Rover out in the woods, and the winner would be the first guy to touch it without being caught by the soldiers that were on patrol trying to find us. I snuck around for a while, crawled along on my belly, heard a twig crack by the side of my head. I froze. I felt like Rambo in *First Blood*.

The soldier walked off.

---

[1] Kirbs is known as one of cricket's most eccentric and endearing characters, and a noted sledger. He once sent Mike Atherton off with the immortal line: 'I've seen better batsmen than you in my fridge…'

I thought I could see the Land Rover so I took my chance and sprinted over towards it. It was pitch black and I misjudged it and ran straight into the door. CLANG...

'Lads,' a disembodied voice shouted. 'We have our winner...'

The furthest I'd ever flown was Cape Town. I got to Adelaide wired and ghosted from the plane, and with an hour's sleep in twenty-four. It was damp and cold. The Academy was in Del Monte, right on the seafront at Henley Beach. I lugged my gear to my room and fell asleep on the floor. I woke up in the same position two hours later. We went straight into a meeting with Rod Marsh, who spent half an hour or so telling us how bloody hard it was going to be. We met his assistants Wayne Phillips and Troy Cooley, and the fitness trainer. He was called Crouchy. He had a mullet haircut with a straight fringe and big Doc Martens on his feet. He was a boxer and as hard as nails. Kirk Russell was out there as our physio. When Rod was done with his intro, Kirk said:

'Quick bit of housekeeping, lads. Robbie Williams is in town. Who wants to go and see him play tonight?'

Great, we thought.

'Who's Robbie Williams?' Rod asked, innocently enough.

In a piss-taking Aussie accent, Graeme Swann replied: 'He's a fucking singer, you ignorant ****.'

Jeez. Swanny had misjudged that one...

Wayne Phillips had to turn his back. He was laughing, but more in shock than anything. Troy walked out of the room.

We waited for the explosion, but Rod just looked at Graeme

for a while, and then ignored him. That was Swanny done in Rod's eyes though.[2]

They spent eight weeks beasting us, trying to break us down physically and mentally. The regime was brutal, six in the morning until seven at night. Rod had a theory that English cricketers were too soft, so he set about putting it right. We lived on the VersaClimbers. We ran the sand dunes, boxed each other, all the hardcore stuff that weeds out the unwilling and the unable. I got so strong. I loved it, loved Crouchy pushing me to the limit.

Fred, Rob Key, Harmi, Nicky Peng and I had a Tuesday Night Club where we'd go out drinking. We had a system. On the way back, we'd stop at the shops and buy a newspaper each, and then stroll back through to our rooms looking as if we'd jumped up early. It didn't occur to us that we were a) drunk and b) still in our nightclub finery. We had some wild ones. I remember Fred handing Nicky and me beers, really insistently:

'Get them down you now...'

We did, or at least we did until we realised that they were warm...

Flintoff was lying on the floor of the bar literally howling with laughter.

---

[2] Swanny's Test career did not blossom until much later, making his debut in 2008. The same cheeky character that so endeared him to fans didn't necessarily help: in addition to the Rod Marsh incident, he'd fallen foul of Duncan Fletcher on the tour of South Africa the previous winter, oversleeping and missing the team bus, and been punched in the face by Darren Gough while standing at a urinal.

'Is this...? Oh Jesus, Fred, it's not, is it...?'

It was.

Unsurprisingly Rod got wind of it and had us up one morning for a five-kilometre run about an hour and half after we'd got into bed. I ran it faster drunk than I could sober. I threw up twice but I didn't care.

He said, 'Look boys, I'll give you enough rope, but if you let me down on the field, you'll be gone, trust me.'

The part I found hardest was the personal development. Every Thursday we would have to stand up in front of the group and speak for a minute about a particular subject. Rod might chuck over a pen and say, 'Talk about that.'

I dreaded it. I would wake up on Monday morning worrying about it. It would overshadow the whole week. I knew that Harmi hated it too. Swanny and Mark Wagh, by contrast, wouldn't shut up. After six weeks, we had to give a five-minute talk on the subject of our choice. As I stood up to do mine, I looked at the front row of the audience and saw Andrew Flintoff, Steve Harmison, Graeme Swann, Rob Key and Alex Tudor, five of the biggest piss-takers you could meet. It was tough, but by the end, I could speak in front of anyone.

I got so strong I was bowling off a six-pace run and still registering 90-plus on the speed gun. Troy began to talk to me about reverse swing. I had the natural speed to bowl it, and the right sort of action to make it work. He talked about the changes in Test cricket, and how the middle overs had become key. Fielding sides needed to be able to get good players out once the ball had got old and soft. Reverse was the best way of doing it. Troy told me to have a mess around with it, and I got it right away. I would bowl in the nets with the worst balls I could find, real old rabbit heads, but I started to make them move in and out at high pace.

I loved it all. I knew that some of the other lads didn't. Swanny was down on the whole experience. Harmi struggled because he missed his home and his family. Sometimes he'd just lie down on the floor during the gym sessions or walk during the runs, but Rod gave him space because he understood what he was going through. To Steve's great credit, he stuck it out, and he went home as fit as he'd ever been. We'd both make our Test debuts the following summer. That winter, we built the bonds that would hold through to 2005 and beyond.

Glamorgan played Derbyshire soon after I got back, and I ran through them. I got 6-40 off the short run. Crofty was almost hit in the throat at first slip when a nick screamed at him. He just got his hands up in time, and told the papers that 'I might have to wear a helmet in the slips for Jones.'

I clean bowled Darren Thomas three balls in a row in the nets with reverse swing, two inners and an away-swinger, and Darren was a proper player. The Glamorgan lads told me I was a different person once I'd been out to Adelaide.

The Sri Lankan touring side came down to Cardiff and I heard that Duncan Fletcher was coming to watch me. When we went out I could see him up on the balcony. I bowled really fast, hit one of their batters and the ball ripped the helmet off his head.

Yet Fletch wasn't happy with my run-up. He felt it was too short and put too much pressure on my body to generate pace. He wanted me to have more momentum. Steve Watkin agreed. Marshy argued that I had rhythm and got through the crease. Fletch won. I knew I'd have to lengthen my run if I wanted to play for England, so I worked with Lynn Davies, the Olympic long-jump champion. We came up with a run that kept me in rhythm but gave me more speed.

David Graveney rang when I was at my mum and dad's place.

'It's good news, mate. You're in the squad – first Test against India at Lord's.'

My dad was hanging his head around the door as I was talking to Grav. He put his thumb up and then down.

I raised mine and smiled.

His face... there are few moments in life like the one where your dad hears you're about to make your Test debut.

Sehwag... Dravid... Tendulkar... Laxman... Ganguly... The names run through my thoughts, recurring, repeating. Proper batsmen, proper players ... They have faced men as fast as me and prospered.

After the joy of selection comes a reckoning. This is what I'd wanted, what I'd craved and strived for. This is what I've got. Now I have to step up, prove myself.

Now or never... Thursday at Lord's...

I worried about it all, my mind on a loop. I worried about where I would sit in the dressing room. I worried about the training and the warm-ups. I worried about who I'd know in the squad.

On my first day with the team at Lord's, Fred was there. Matthew Hoggard I'd seen around. The rest of the side I barely knew from Adam. They were internationals, separate from the rest, occupying the space where I wanted to be: Alec Stewart, Graham Thorpe, Michael Vaughan, Mark Butcher, Ashley Giles, the captain Nasser Hussain...

And when I pushed open the dressing-room door and looked around, there was no space. I felt like the kid from the Glamorgan second XI knocking on the first-teamers' door.

Alec Stewart was in the far corner. 'Hey, mate, come and change over here...' He shifted his things and made some space.

I think Stewie regretted it after a couple of days when he realised how messy I was. Not as bad as Flintoff, but not great, and Alec was famously neat, his kit immaculately kept, his whites creaseless, his street clothes as crisp as his timing with the bat. It was a big occasion for the Gaffer, because it was his 119th Test cap, the all-time record for an Englishman, and yet he made sure that I felt welcome.

There was a new kit bag for me, full of pristine gear still in cellophane. All that was missing was the cap. That would only come if I was selected for the game. Gough and Caddick were injured, Hoggard, Flintoff and Craig White nailed on, so the final bowling spot was between me and Dominic Cork.

I was pretty sure I'd play. We had the team meeting that would become so familiar. I said nothing, just listened. I'd never bowled to Tendulkar. What did I have to say about getting him out?

I worried about the Tuesday practice. How much should

I bowl? I worried about Wednesday. When would I know if I was playing? Hoggy sorted me out. 'Have a good bowl on Tuesday, forty-five minutes or so, and then an over or two out in the middle on Wednesday to get used to the slope.'

It came out well. If they had any doubts about choosing me, maybe they disappeared on Tuesday when I let one go and it swung late and almost cleaned up a wicketkeeper on the ground staff who was helping out. He just got his glove on it as it rose at his forehead. Bob Cottam, who was one of the bowling coaches, told me two years later that it was the fastest ball he'd ever seen.

Craig White looked after me. I think he saw a bit of himself in me: quiet, shy. There were no cliques in the team, but a lot of the lads who'd been together for a long time would go to dinner or out somewhere. I sat in my room. There was a knock at the door and behind it was Craig, holding pizza he'd been out and bought himself.

At practice on Wednesday, Dominic Cork walked over and shook my hand. 'Congratulations, mate,' he said.

That's how I found out I was playing. Corky had been released from the squad and wanted to wish me well.

I went back to my room again that night. There was a knock on the door. It was Craig. 'Let's go to the bar,' he said. 'It'll settle you down.'

It settled me down a bit too much. We must have had six or seven pints of Stella – or at least I did. I felt great. And then in the morning I didn't.

I'd have been okay to bowl, but it wasn't ideal. My head was still zinging when Nasser handed over my cap. Fortunately, the coin fell Nasser's way and we batted all day and into the next. Well, Nasser did, making 150-odd, while everyone else chipped in.

I walked onto a Test match ground for the first time when Ashish Nehra bowled Ashley Giles. England's number ten. Down the stairs and through the gate and out to an ovation I barely heard. Craig was batting well at the other end, which helped. So did the fact that we already had 390 on the board.

'Just watch the ball, mate,' he said, 'and try to get me on strike.'

That went out the window pretty quickly. I just tried to hit it as hard as I could. Zaheer Khan went back over his head for six. I saw Craig at the other end laughing. The crowd loved it. I carved away merrily and ended up with 44 from 43 deliveries, seven fours and a six. Not bad.[3]

Matthew Hoggard knocked over Wasim Jaffer in the first over, but by the time I came to bowl, Sehwag and Dravid were set. It was hot, the wicket was more like an Indian dustbowl than an English deck. What little I recall of that first spell now are sense memories: the heat, oppressive and still, the nerves, so many more than when I batted, Nasser urging me on, the first ball coming out at 89 mph . . . rushing a couple of high-class batsmen.

My second spell is clearer. India lost Sehwag and then Nehra quickly. Tendulkar came in and Nasser brought me back to bowl to him. I was struck right away by his size.

---

[3] My 44 was the equal-highest score by a Glamorgan player in Tests for England, along with Hugh Morris's 44 against West Indies at the Oval in 1991. This makes me very happy.

He was tiny, but his bat looked huge, as broad as a barn door. I bowled quick, 90-plus, and he pushed forward as if he had all day to play it.

I asked Nasser if I could go around the wicket to him. The ball was dry and shiny. I thought, 'Yeah, this is me.' I dug one in at his ribs and he almost dragged it on. I shaped a couple into him and then went across with the angle and he nicked it to Graham Thorpe at second slip, who dropped it.

It hurt, but I knew at that moment that I was good enough. If I could do it to Tendulkar, I could do it to anyone.

It was five days of exhilaration and exhaustion, tinged with un-reality. We won comfortably, by 170 runs. My first wicket came later in that first innings. I knocked over Ajay Ratra, and what I remember most is the relief and joy on Nasser Hussain's face. I got Agit Agarkar soon afterwards, and in the second innings came my first really big wickets: Sehwag bowled with a reversing inswinger to which he shouldered arms, and later Laxman when he was batting freely. The only cloud was a niggling rib injury caused by my bowling arm continually colliding with a sore spot on my side, but on the way back to Cardiff, I slept a deep and contented sleep for the first time in a week. The experience had drained me utterly. It wasn't until it was over that I realised the pressure and the stress that I'd been under – much of it self-imposed – but now I knew, as the car headed west, that I was an international cricketer.

I knew too that, because of my side injury, I'd miss the next Test, which was just a week later, and soon Andy Caddick would be fit again. I'd have to wait, but not too long.

*

Of that first Academy group, Steve Harmison and Alex Tudor would also play against India. On the Ashes tour that followed in the winter, where I would be so badly injured in the First Test at Brisbane, Harmison and Owais Shah were selected in the original touring party and Alex Tudor and Rob Key went out as replacements. By 2004, the summer that Andrew Strauss and Ian Bell made their debuts, the Academy had become the National Cricket Performance Centre and had moved to a permanent location at Loughborough. The England A team was rebranded as the England Lions. Age-group, Academy and Lions teams played domestically during the summers and toured during the winters. Central contracts, which had begun in 2000, grew in their availability and range, meaning that players moved upwards as employees of the ECB rather than their counties – and were effectively full-time internationals. Under Duncan and Nasser, and then Duncan and Michael Vaughan, we slowly left the shattered, splintered 1990s behind.[4]

A new culture was forming and hardening and I was on the inside of it. The culture gradually became known as the England 'bubble'. Life inside the bubble became increasingly rarefied. Everything was taken care of: from kit to travel arrangements, we had the best of everything. The money, the perks, the

---

[4] Research from Sheffield Hallam University on the central contract system showed that between 1987 and 1999, England made 368 changes to their Test side in just 130 matches and won only 20 per cent of them. Between 2000 and 2012, they made 263 changes in 166 matches and won 45 per cent of them. The system really helped me: once you're on contract, you feel very much a part of things, and a lot of worry and stress over selection drops away. I think you play better that way.

lifestyle were, from the outside, deeply enviable. There is no doubt that the notion of the bubble improved English cricket – after the eighteen-year wait to 2005, England won three of the next four Ashes series, a Twenty20 World Cup and became the number-one ranked Test match team. Life inside the bubble became more relentless, with most of the year spent in hotels, training and playing, training and playing.... Careers became more intense and were shortened by it. Psychological problems followed. Players finished their careers far richer than before, but also burned out and frazzled by it all.

Yet there was one thing worse than being inside the bubble, and that was being outside it. Once you left the bubble, life would become far more chaotic and uncertain.

5. Old Trafford

In which I run through the enemy for the first time, discover that pain doesn't always go away, and partake of a little too much of a sponsor's product...

Twelve hours after Geraint held the catch that won the Edgbaston Test, he watches as I give his wife Jen a piggyback down a street outside the Walkabout pub and dive a lot less successfully than he did. I charge along for a bit and then faceplant – the alcohol numbs any pain. Jen shrieks but survives the fall.

We're all together, the whole team, wives, girlfriends and a great group of fans, and we are all steaming drunk: it seems like the only plausible reaction to a game like that one. What else is there to say about it? Even the Australians who've been hardened by the intensity of series after series that they are expected to win (and usually do) were saying they'd never played in anything like it.

People say that it's harder to watch a match like that than it is to play in it. I disagree. The tension and angst and stress have to go somewhere. You need to get them out of the body, out of the mind and the nerves. The chance that I dropped near the end hadn't mattered – in fact it set up the stranger-than-fiction grand finale – but the long, dreadful minutes when I thought that it would matter are still exacting their toll somewhere in body and mind.

Fletch sent us out for a drink. He knew we'd be doing it anyway I suppose, but he could tell that we needed a release.

The Old Trafford Test starts in four days, and we're young guys. The hangover, when it comes, is big but worth it.

Matt Maynard drives us back to Wales. I chill for a day or so. The ankle is still sore – the alcohol certainly doesn't help with that, but it's a trade-off. A bit of pain for a bit of peace. However, it seems to be getting more painful rather than less. I ring Kirk.

'Can I have another jab?'

'No, mate. We can't do that. The cortisone should last.'

'Then we better find some strong painkillers.'

Talking to Kirk relaxes me nonetheless. Pain I can't control panics me, but he's right, I can get through Old Trafford and then there is a break during which I can rest it and manage the inflammation. Maybe they'll let me have another jab then. Maybe it'll stay just on the right side of the pain register. All I want to do is keep playing in this series. I don't think it's too much to ask, given what I've been through. The thought of not playing makes me feel sad, angry, resentful. We've all been waiting for this summer for too long.

*

We get to Old Trafford with three days to go. From the moment I arrive at the hotel I feel as though people are looking at how I'm walking, checking if there's a limp. I get into stubborn mode, show no weakness. When we have the hard Tuesday session, it actually starts to feel okay, better than it did at Edgbaston. Kirk reckons that the cortisone is really kicking in now. After a few days off the booze, the alcohol has flushed from my system too. I take my pills, run in hard and the ball comes out well.

I can't wait to play at Old Trafford, can't bloody wait because it's the best ground for fast bowlers in the country, and the wicket looks great. It's rock hard, slightly patchy in colour, the surface abrasive. Old Trafford has a wide square and a lush outfield, and I know that we'll be able to get the ball reversing. Wickets fall on this ground, and that's just as well. It always rains here too, and you can almost guarantee that you'll lose a couple of sessions to the weather so the game needs to keep moving along. For now though, that brown, hard pitch bakes under the sun.

Buchanan is playing his mind games with the Australian training sessions, going in the nets when we're supposed to have them, using different sections of the ground. Fletch gets us together. 'Boys,' he says. 'They're worried. You're young, hungry and fearless and they've never faced that.'

We can feel it too, this change in mood. At Edgbaston after the match, Matty Hayden came and sat with me and talked about the game. It was the usual player chit-chat, albeit about an extraordinary match, but there was something different about him. Humble is the wrong word, but I'm not sure of the right one; I think he had spent his career looking at England one way, and was now beginning to see us in another. Things that used to happen to us have started happening to them, those unlucky, dumb, unpredictable things that change matches and change series, that make you feel as if you're on a downward curve despite all the sweat and effort you're putting in, despite doing all the things that you usually do and that usually work: there have been the T20 defeat; the loss to Bangladesh, Bristol, the loss to Somerset; the first morning at Lord's; Edgbaston; the toss; the rumoured row between Ponting and Warne; Glenn McGrath tripping over a ball someone should have picked up but didn't.

Then, on the Monday night before Old Trafford, Brett Lee is admitted to hospital with an infection in his knee.

Lee stays in hospital for two nights, and gets out the day before the Test. They must have been working on McGrath's ankle all day every day, because he's at the ground and the rumour is he'll play.

Lee and McGrath come out for the final Australian training session the afternoon before the game. They do some sprints and other light drills with Errol Alcott, the Australian physio. They look okay. Lee is passed fit right away. McGrath is going to wait until Thursday morning before making a decision on his ankle.

We reckon that they'll risk him. Kasper and Gillespie went the distance at Edgbaston, and they have only one other quick bowler in the squad, a guy called Shaun Tait, who is twenty-two years old, a fast, wild kid from South Australia who has never played a Test and who has a reputation for drawing blood: he supposedly felled Ponting in the nets in Sri Lanka on his first tour, and broke the West Australia keeper's foot with a yorker. However, when he came to England to play for Durham at the end of last summer he lost his run-up,[1] and there is no telling how the pressure of an Ashes Test may affect him. Buchanan and Ponting must be concerned because they've called up Stuart Clark, who's been playing county cricket at Middlesex, as cover. He's another very good bowler, but not one our batters would lose sleep over.

My guess is McGrath will do what all fast bowlers who are 85 per cent fit would do: play. Strap it up, swallow the pills and grin and bear it. In an ideal world, he would not have to, but the world, for Australia, is not quite as ideal as it once was.

We want to compound their discomfort, to keep banging home our message: we have batsmen that score; bowlers that take wickets; players that work as a team, that graft for each other.

Luck gets more luck. Vaughan wins the toss, for just the second time in twelve. On a morning of high cloud that slowly breaks open with patches of blue, we bat first. Lee plays. McGrath plays. I imagine how he would have been urging Ponting to win the toss, hoping for Australia to bat and for his ankle to have one more day of treatment, but it is not to be. Not for Australia and not for McGrath, not right now at Old Trafford. Instead, *I* get a day off, another day to watch England bat and bat...

---

[1] On his debut for Durham against Somerset, Tait had bowled twenty-one no-balls and two wides in his twelve overs; six overs against Essex went for 63. He returned to Australia early by mutual consent. His coach at Durham, Martyn Moxon, even tried having Tait run in with his eyes closed, a technique that encourages a bowler to take off into his delivery stride when it feels entirely natural. Our bowling coach Troy Cooley once used the same tactic with Hoggy, who quickly regained his rhythm.

From the fifth ball of McGrath's third over, he draws the edge of Trescothick's bat, but Adam Gilchrist drops the chance.

Brett Lee hits Andrew Strauss on the helmet and then bowls him soon afterwards with a terrific slower ball.

Michael Vaughan comes in. He has made 32 runs in four innings in the series. He has been clean bowled three times. McGrath has targeted him – his usual policy of cutting the head off the snake.

As Vaughan takes guard, Ponting gives him heaps from second slip.

Vaughan says: 'You're no Steve Waugh, mate…'

It shuts the Australians up. It lets Ponting know that Vaughan's mind is clear and sharp.

He and Trescothick score freely until the lunch break, Vaughan reaching 41, Trescothick 35.

From the second ball of McGrath's second over after lunch, Vaughan edges an attempted cut shot high and hard to Gilchrist's right. He drops the chance. With the next, Vaughan is clean bowled by a tremendous nip-backer that cartwheels his off stump – but Steve Bucknor's arm is out before the stump has come to rest, the call of 'No-ball' causing McGrath to bow his head and put his hand over his face as Edgbaston erupts into a joyous, Australia-baiting cheer.

A day that might have been Australia's will now be ours. A day that might have been Glenn McGrath's will instead be Michael Vaughan's.

McGrath toughs out three more overs on that ankle, the stiff and sore and strapped-up ankle that in all probability changes his rock-solid stride pattern and causes the no-ball. Vaughan hits him for consecutive boundaries and Ponting takes him off.

Warne and Lee come on, Warne with 599 Test match wickets to his name. Trescothick carts him through midwicket. Vaughan punches him through the covers. We reach 163-1, and then it happens, this piece of history. Tres looks to hit Warne through the leg side once more, but this time the ball stays low and ping-pongs from pad to glove to something else and loops up to Gilchrist, who can't drop this one, and Warne is the first man in history to 600 wickets.[2] Ever the showman, he doffs his sunhat to all sides of the ground.

That's all they get though. Belly settles in with Vaughan. Warne has used up his magic – temporarily at least. Lee and McGrath are short of fitness. Gillespie is short of wickets, and so after forty-five overs of day one, Ponting turns to the left-arm wrist spin of Simon Katich, a man who has bowled less than 100 overs in his Test career.

Bell and Vaughan milk him until tea, with England at 195-2 and the skipper on 93 not out, riding his luck, making them pay.

After the break Warne resumes around the wicket to two right-handers, the tactic he uses when he feels attritional rather than attacking. Vaughan clips his first ball to the boundary. Warne forces him to kick the rest away, playing on the nerves of a man

---

[2] Come the end of that first day at Old Trafford, Warnie had bowled more than 45,500 deliveries in Test matches alone, and what remained perhaps most amazing was his accuracy – he'd conceded just 2.6 runs per over across his career. A month short of his thirty-sixth birthday, having overcome serious shoulder and finger injuries, and having been part of a team that often played so well that wickets were shared around, it was an extraordinary moment.

who is 99 not out, but Vaughan has been there and done it and he sucks it up and takes his time and when he gets on strike to Glenn McGrath he clips him for three through midwicket and the captain has his moment, he makes his statement. McGrath has not cut the head from the snake, not here, not today. He has bowled bravely on his crooked ankle, but his pace is down and his mood is dark and getting darker with every over. He is chuntering and sighing, his head bowed, reading the signs, reading the signals.

And the signals for Australia are all bad. McGrath comes off and Gillespie comes on, and he is short of confidence and short of pace, perhaps sensing that the end is near for him.

Vaughan pulls his second ball high into the stands for six and then cuts the next for four. In Gillespie's next he loses his line and Vaughan clips him for two, then four through midwicket. In the next, Vaughan thumps him through square leg for four more, and then Bell inside-edges an attempted yorker for another. Vaughan hits the first three balls of Gillespie's next over for four, driving him straight twice and pulling the other, to go past 150.

Ponting has no choice but to take Gillespie off. He has bowled eighteen deliveries to Vaughan. They have gone for 34 runs. Vaughan has cleaned him out, maybe finished him. It's dramatic, and the crowd are basking in it, but there is something sad about it too. Gillespie has been a great bowler in a great team, but something is missing now, an edge that may not come back. All Test cricketers live with the knowledge that what makes them special can be small and finite, and they understand that one day it will be them having time tapping on their shoulder.

The game can be cruel. Ponting brings Katich back on, and

Vaughany somehow hits a pie of a full toss right down Glenn McGrath's throat to fall for 166, his fourth Ashes hundred, this one the equal of any of the three he struck on his golden tour of Australia in 2002–3[3] and, as the first on either side in this series, probably more important, too. We are still fifteen overs from the close of day one, but the game is already moving away from Australia.

Kev, who for some reason has changed the colour of the Dead Skunk streak in his hair from white to blue, piles on a quick 43 with Belly, but then tries for one big shot too many and is caught on the fence hooking at Brett Lee. Hoggy goes in as nightwatchman to see out the day, but falls to the very last delivery, another rocket at the end of a hostile spell from Lee. It gives a slightly false feel to the score, but there is no doubt who has the upper hand now.

England 341-5, Vaughan 166, Trescothick 63, Bell 59 not out; Lee 2-58.

Day two
Bell falls early on the second morning. Manchester rain comes and then goes. Fred and Geraint blast forty-odd each. Ponting gives Gillespie an over at Steve Harmison. Harmi launches him over mid-on for a one-bounce four. Warnie bowls me for a

---

[3] In the five Tests of the 2002–3 Ashes (after I'd gone home injured) Vaughany made 633 runs, including centuries in Adelaide (177), Melbourne (145) and Sydney (183). In all he had scored 1,481 runs in the calendar year of 2002, which took him to the top of the ICC Test rankings for batting, the first Englishman since Graham Gooch to get there. He succeeded Nasser Hussain as England captain in the summer of 2003.

duck three balls later and we're done, 444 all out. Nelsons[4] are supposed to be unlucky scores for us, but we're pretty happy with this one.

It's a particular triumph for Vaughany, who had been under the pump, the pressure of captaincy having taken the gilt from the great rush of form that had made him such a formidable Test match batsman for the past three years. What's amazing is not that he has made such a big and significant hundred – he's too good a player not to come back – but that he has remained the same character throughout, although you can probably quadruple the pressure that we are feeling when it comes to what he's dealing with. I remember bowling to him in a county game a couple of years ago, when Yorkshire were going for the county championship. I bowled very quickly that day, and I went after him from the start. He took me on. I hit him on the gloves a couple of times, he hooked a couple and all he did was smile at me. As a quick bowler that's the worst thing. You want to feel as though you are having an impact, physically and psychologically, but with Michael it was impossible to know. He seemed unflappable then, and he is even more so now. It's a great advantage for us in the dressing room – inscrutable Fletcher and imperturbable Vaughan.

*

---

[4] 'Nelsons' are scores of 111, 222 etc. and are considered by England to be 'unlucky' numbers on which wickets may fall. The late and much-loved umpire David Shepherd would hop on one leg until the Nelson passed. The origins of the phrase are obscure but probably refer to the old saying that Nelson had 'one arm, one eye and one ambition'. Australia's equivalent number is 87, supposedly unlucky because it is thirteen short of a hundred. Players in both dressing rooms observe certain traditions when these numbers are noticed.

The swinging cricket ball, delivered at pace, has a mystery to it that the spinning ball does not. Warne and Muralitharan and Saqlain and their ilk may have many clever variations of wrist and finger, but they have mystique rather than mystery. They deceive batsmen, but what they do is explainable, and demonstrable. The ball spins in the direction that they have spun it. By contrast swing and its more recent companion reverse swing has a genuine mystery that has led to mystique, misinformation and far darker rumour.

Science still struggles to entirely explain the swinging ball, in cricket and in its kissing cousin baseball. The basic principles are sound. In cricket, conventional swing happens when one side of the ball is shinier (and therefore smoother) than the other, and travels through the air fractionally faster, thus moving the ball in the direction that the shiny side is headed. The bowler can control the swing by gripping the ball down the seam, with the shiny side to the right if they want it to move away from the right-handed batsman and to the left if they want to move it in.

Yet the basic principles do not explain why the ball swings on some grounds and not others, in some weather conditions and not others, for some bowlers and not others. It doesn't explain why a particular bowler can swing one ball and not the next, can swing it out but not in, or in but not out, or at high pace but not slower and so on, ad infinitum.

We all have our theories and superstitions. Particular manufacturers produce balls more likely to swing. Darker, smaller balls swing more than redder, lighter ones. The red ball swings more than the white ball. Balls manufactured by Duke's swing more than balls manufactured by Kookaburra.

Balls with a prominent seam swing more than balls with a flatter seam. Cloud makes it swing. Humidity makes it swing. Micro-climates make it swing. Position of the arm and position on the crease make it swing, as does the position of the seam. Ultimately, this evidence is anecdotal. A swing bowler is always at the mercy of external factors.

There's a scientist at NASA who has been studying swing and its variants for twenty-five years. If NASA scientists have to write a paper to explain what happens and why, then there's not much chance of your average fast bowler understanding the physics of it all.

Yet it is the bowlers who nurture it and improve it and sometimes even reinvent it. The notion of another kind of swing began to emerge from Pakistan in the late 1970s, a kind of swing that did not depend on the ball being new and in good condition, because keeping a ball in the state necessary for conventional swing was impossible in Pakistan with its abrasive pitches and dry outfields. Instead, bowlers noticed that when the ball was in a certain condition, with one side more rough and scuffed than the other, it would begin to swing *towards* the rough side when bowled above a certain pace. It seemed counter-intuitive, but Sarfraz passed the technique down to Imran, who showed Wasim and Waqar, who perfected it and began destroying the world's batsmen with dramatic, unplayable late swing bowled at searing pace. So revolutionary did it seem that they were accused, in dark whispers, of ball-tampering, accusations that didn't really disappear until the rest of the world understood how to reverse swing the ball too.

Troy showed me how to do it at the Academy. It suited my

game. I had the raw pace to get the kind of late movement that deceives good batsmen. I learned how to reverse it not just into the right-handed batsman – the easiest delivery to bowl – but to move it away, too. And I learned how disciplined the team has to be to get the ball into the right condition quickly.

Tres is our ball manager. It's a vital role. It means the ball goes to him when Geraint's taken it or it's been thrown in, and he will work on the condition of it, mainly ensuring that it is kept as dry as possible, and that one side retains whatever smoothness and shine he can get on it, while the other is allowed to deteriorate. Apart from Tres and the bowlers, very few others handle the ball, especially the lads who get sweaty hands. Sweat on the dry part of the ball will delay the arrival of reverse swing. When fielders throw the ball in, they know to bounce it into the square before it reaches Geraint, because that will rough it up and dry it out even more.

If we look after the ball properly, we can sometimes get it reversing after twenty or thirty overs. It's a massive advantage, because it means that there's only a small gap between the new ball swinging and the older ball starting to as well.

The other thing we do well is choose the right ball. In Test cricket, before the start of each innings, one player from the fielding side can choose the new ball from a box of twelve. Sometimes Harmi chooses, sometimes I do, sometimes Fred. This summer's batch of Duke's balls are quite dark. We like to go for the darkest, and one that feels small in the hand. The darker the ball, the harder it is for the batsman to spot which side is which once it starts reversing. This is important because if a batsman can pick you from the hand, it reduces your advantage. Wasim used to run in with one hand covering the ball, something Fred has started doing, but I don't bother. The Australians don't seem to be able to pick me anyway.

Today will be the day that reverse swing makes its mark. Today will be my day, this match will be my match. That is my mindset from the first ball I bowl, which comes after twelve overs of Australia's first innings, twelve overs in which Langer and Hayden have put on 52 runs, 26 to Langer, 25 to Hayden, and right away it's coming out well. I have rhythm immediately, the ankle feels good and I'm right at Matty Hayden again, the third delivery a fast yorker that spears across him and he does well to dig out, the fourth a rapid short one that slaps into his pads and has us roaring out a big appeal that Billy Bowden turns down.

Vaughany has a hunch that Gilo should be on, and so he moves me from the Pavilion End to the Stretford End, and it's Gilo who does it for us and opens them up, who has Justin Langer advancing down the wicket to his fifth delivery and clipping him hard towards midwicket from an inside edge, an edge that Ian Bell at short leg somehow plucks from the air one-handed, a miracle catch that sends us into tea on a high, that sends them into tea with one of their big guns down and the feeling that when we really need it, things go our way.

I can't wait to get back out there, can't bloody wait for the clock to tick through the next twenty minutes so that I can bowl at Matthew Hayden and Ricky Ponting. When I do, I hit it hard right away, no loosener, no gentle leave ball for Ponting to get his eye back in; instead I run in fast for that first ball after tea and hit the back of a length, from where the ball kicks up high, hits the shoulder of his bat as he looks to push forward and loops gently to Ian Bell, a catch as gentle as his first was instinctive.

'You beauty!'

Ponting out... Ponting gone... first ball after tea.

The captain of England makes 166. The captain of Australia makes 7.

The head of the snake.

This is a huge moment for me, a massive wicket. When I watch the footage back later, I barely recognise myself: head shaved down to the bone, mad-eyed, arms waving. It feels odd, almost as though it's not me. I imagine what it must look like from Ricky Ponting's end... this thing running towards him. The slips charging at him from behind... Jeez.

I'm pumped now, fucking pumped, and I spear in at Damien Martyn and give him a short, straight one that he does well to stay on top of. In the next over it happens: the ball starts to reverse. We've only bowled twenty-one overs with it, but I feel it begin. The first slides way down the leg side and swings late past Geraint's dive for four byes. The next dips in to Hayden's pads.

I plan to go full and fast with the next but I get my release point infinitesimally wrong and at my pace that's all it takes: the ball flies chest-high towards Hayden, but luckily for him and for me it's wide as well as high and it disappears to the boundary for five no-balls. I apologise to Haydos and the umpire.

Steve Bucknor gives me a warning: if I deliver another, then I won't be allowed to bowl again this innings.

I go full and straight again with more late shape and get it right this time. I pin Hayden on the pad and we have another good shout knocked back by Steve Bucknor. I shove the next too far across him, but again it reverses. Maybe this plays on his mind. Maybe things are just less certain now. When he is on strike at the other end, he decides to move forward to Gilo's looping slow left arm but then stays back instead. The ball skids low out of the rough and traps him on the crease and Hayden watches Billy's crooked finger rise up towards the sky.

Brilliant from Gilo and Hayden is gone in the thirties again, 34 this time, and still the doubt...

Vaughany spells me. The ankle's sore but I'm pleased with 8-3-18-1.

Fred takes my place and with the first ball after the drinks break, coming around the wicket, he reverses a booming inswinger at Simon Katich who misreads it completely and shoulders arms, the ball detonating his off stump from the ground. Superb from Flintoff. Superb from Tres the ball manager. The Australians aren't picking the reverse swing at all.

At the other end, Gilo is magnificent too. With the third ball of his eleventh over, he rips a big spinner out of the footmarks, across the face of Damien Martyn's bat and into the stumps.

Marto's wicket is in ruins. Australia's innings is in ruins, too, or very nearly, at 133-5 and with Shane Warne and Adam Gilchrist at the crease. Both are batting a place higher than usual because Michael Clarke's back has gone and no one is certain whether he will bat at all in this innings. He hasn't travelled to the ground this morning. Instead he's in bed at the hotel, waiting by the phone.

Fred thunders in to Gilchrist. Since he came into Test cricket at the end of 1999, Gilchrist has been a puzzle that the bowlers of the world cannot solve. Before this summer, he had made over 5,000 runs at an average of more than 55, scored at a strike rate of 83.26 runs per 100 balls, which is faster than Lara, faster than Ponting, faster than everyone, and he's done it all batting at number seven, coming in just when the bowlers have finished working their way through the legends that bat above him.

He has an unusual method, with his hands right at the top of the bat handle. He sometimes holds a squash ball in his bottom hand to make sure he's not choking the bat, which he swings hard, with long levers. He has no fear, no doubt in going for his shots, and he goes for them from ball one. He hits the ball in unusual areas: he'll take a ball from outside off stump and whack it into the stands over midwicket; he'll flay length balls through cover; he'll carve anything short and wide; he's got this flip off his pads that looks effortless but that pings the ball miles over long-leg. He's used to opening in one-day cricket, so he doesn't fear the new ball. I find him difficult, really difficult, and he's one of the players that we've spoken the most about.

He's never been worked out, never been stopped, not so far, but maybe Flintoff is cracking the code. He bowls around the wicket and reverses it away from the bat, something that he can do with his action, but that I would find very hard, and he got him twice at Lord's, nicked off and bowled.

Now he thunders in and hurries Gilchrist into a half-hearted scoop that falls just short of Ian Bell. Next he bowls a rapid, reversing yorker that Gilchrist just manages to drop those high hands on. Then a wide one, moving away, drawing the drive and Gilchrist obliges, only for Kev to grass a half-chance at short-cover.

Australia are rocking but they hold on. Warne makes sure he gets on strike to Flintoff, while Gilly takes Giles. It's smart cricket, even though Warne has to take some ferocious short stuff.

Warnie is a much better player than he looks. His technique is odd: he barely picks the bat up and he doesn't have much of a follow-through either, but his hands and wrists and forearms are so strong the ball just rockets from his bat. He plays from unusual positions too: he'll walk across the crease and hit through the leg side, and then stay leg side to carve through off. He's never made a Test hundred, but he knows he can, and he wants one.

Australia could use it too. Together Warne and Gilchrist see Flintoff off and keep Gilo out. We take drinks. Harmi comes back in place of Fred. Warne whacks him for four. Gilchrist carves him for another. Warne runs down the wicket to Gilo and hits him for a one-bounce boundary back over his head. The score reaches 190. The pressure begins to ease just a little. Vaughan rolls his shoulders at me. I get loose, stretch, feel out the ankle, which is buzzing and sore. Can't think about it though, can't let it stop me, because the ball is coming out well today.

It's Gilchrist on strike. I look at the board. He has made 30. 'He's in,' I tell myself, 'so go hard, no loosener. Push it across him, get him playing.'

The ankle burns as soon as I start my run-up but I don't care about that. I'm here to graft. We all are. What I care about is getting this first ball to Gilchrist where I want it, and I do. It's full and quick and moving across the stumps, and he doesn't move his feet at all, instead he just swings his arms and it seems to hit an old part of the wicket and jag away from him, catching the edge as it does.

BANG! First ball! That's another big wicket for me, to add to Ponting's, and the lads are all over me because it's the wicket we wanted, the wicket we needed, and all eyes are on the dressing rooms to see who comes out.

And it's Clarke, with his bad back and Matt Hayden as his runner. Clarke, who has been summoned to the ground from his hotel room because Australia are getting desperate here.

I feel a great surge go through me. The ground is electric. Australia are rocking, and Clarke is mine, I know it, and I think he knows it too. I feel as though I can get him out when I want, because his faults fit my strengths. I really want to get after him, get in his face . . . bowl full and straight, because he's a walking wicket for LBW early on. He likes to step across his stumps to work through midwicket, but when his timing is slightly out he plays across his front pad. Anything that moves late can do him.

You have your bunnies and he is one of mine. I know I'm in his head.

In *my* head is this: 'Bowl where you normally bowl, top of off, bring it back and it's a matter of time.' It sounds arrogant but it's not. It's just the reality of it.

Clarke knows it's coming, too. He's fidgeting on the crease. I see his feet are going as I run in.

It takes me twelve balls. I beat him outside off stump. I give him a bouncer that gets called wide. He drives me a couple of times, once quite sweetly. His back is bad and he's not hanging around. He's here to take me on.

As I turn around to walk back to my mark I say to Fred, who's at mid-off: '*Pel araf.*' It's Welsh for 'slower ball'.

'Don't know what you're on about, pal, just bowl it,' says Fred.

I do.

Fletch is always telling me, 'When you bowl your slower one, hang it out there, sixth stump line, even seventh.'[5] My slower ball is an off-spinner. I put my thumb on the side of the ball and roll it out, hopefully with no real change of arm speed. Sometimes it will really grip and move.

It comes out perfectly, nice and wide and full, and Clarke's eyes light up – something to hit – but he's through the shot too early and it spoons up off the bottom of the blade to bucket-hands Flintoff, who bags it.

He grabs me. '*Pel araf…* slower ball,' I yell in his ear.

Fred smiles.

England 444; Australia 214-7, Warne 45 not out; SP Jones 3-30, Giles 3-65. England lead by 230 runs.

Day three

As they always have and always will at Old Trafford, the rains blow in and take time out of the game. They arrive at 7 a.m., come down steadily through the morning, and only start to

---

[5] The terms 'fourth stump', 'fifth stump' and so on are simply ways for me to picture the line on which I want to bowl, the fourth stump being an imaginary 'extra' stump outside the off stump, the fifth stump a second, and so on. The gap between the stumps is a standard three inches, so a ball delivered on a fourth-stump line would miss the off stump by that margin.

clear in the early afternoon. By the time the ground staff have worked their magic – they are the real rain men here – we'll have a maximum of thirty-eight overs in the day.

Vaughan and Fletch want these last three Australian wickets sharpish so that we can pile on the runs and have the time to knock them over again. They need another 31 to avoid the follow-on, but I don't think it's an option for us anyway.

We push hard, perhaps too hard, and Warne scythes away and quickly knocks off the follow-on target. He gets two lives, one either side of yet more rain. Geraint misses a stumping chance from Gilo and, perhaps rattled, grasses an edge off Flintoff. It happens in cricket. We rally around him, pick him up, because we're a team and we're strong, and no one will feel worse about it than Geraint – not Gilo, not Fred, not Vaughany, not anyone. I remember how he bailed me out with that heart-stopping catch to dismiss Kasper and win the Edgbaston Test.

Warne and Gillespie hold firm. Time is gone from the game, and maybe Warnie is thinking of that elusive Test hundred, a cool, cool cat with all those lives.

At close of play Fletch tells the press conference that Jonah's misses didn't matter because we'd have batted again regardless of whether Australia had passed the follow-on target.

When we're back in the rooms, someone says that, for the first time in twenty years, England are the bookmakers' favourites to win the Ashes.

Australia 264-7, Warne 78 not out; SP Jones 3-43, Giles 3-90. England lead by 180 runs.

*

Day four

The *Mail On Sunday* has run the story about Ponting's bust-up with Warne at Edgbaston. They call it 'a stand-up row'. They say that Adam Gilchrist had to break it up. Fletch has banned the newspapers, but we hear and we see. All the press is going our way, joining the bookmakers and the crowds and the TV viewing figures. Geoff Lawson, one of Australia's battery of retired fiery, plain-speaking quicks, writes that Hayden, Ponting and Gilchrist need to start scoring some runs against decent bowling, rather than the 'medium pace' that they've become accustomed to in the last few years (there isn't a fast bowler alive of course, that doesn't think the bowling was quicker in their day...). England's 1981 Ashes winning captain Mike Brearley writes about our 'potent' reverse swing. Australian writer Peter English notes sarcastically that the fourteen overs possible yesterday were 'Australia's best day of the past two Tests'. Former Australian opening bat turned commentator Michael Slater asks 'if they [Australia] are practising with enough intensity'. Peter Roebuck of the *Sydney Morning Herald* writes that Jason Gillespie 'is a spent force'.

These are the signs and the signals that we have been transmitting. We don't have to think about them, don't have to worry, just focus and everything else will take care of itself.

My ankle is sore but okay. Yesterday's rain had its upside for me.

I have to wait for six overs to get the ball in my hand, three from Fred and three from Harmi, six overs in which Warne gets his score up to 86.

I've been fielding at fine leg and copping it from a lone Australian loudmouth who's sitting in with the England fans.

'Where's your missus gone, Jones? Oh yeah, you haven't got one any more...'

'Oi, Jones, how's your knee...?'

A couple of the English lads get on his back, but I turn around and tell them not to bother. This idiot's firing me up nicely. I'll shut him up.

Fred comes off and I come on. I get the first delivery badly wrong, short and wide and Warne carves it hard to the point boundary to go to 90.

Fuck it.

I decide to try to force him back, set him up for something full and straight, but the next delivery is wrong again, too full and sliding into his hitting area, and he *does* hit it, flat and hard and straight to Gilo, who is a few yards in from the square leg fence. He only has to move about two steps to bag the catch.

Warne throws his head back. He can't believe he's just given away a hundred. He hit that ball as well as he could too. A yard either side and it's a certain boundary. The longed-for century has escaped him.[6]

The lads pile on but I'm not happy.

'Fuck's sake, Simon, that's a shit ball,' I shout. I can't help it. It's an odd part of my nature but I don't like taking wickets with bad deliveries. It almost feels as though I've cheated the game. I'd rather bowl the ball again and get it right, regardless of whether it takes a wicket or not.

---

[6] A Test match hundred would be one of the few achievements denied to Shane Warne. His best remained the 99 he made against New Zealand at the WACA in 2001. I'm still glad I got him out though.

Vaughany is quick to pull me up. He grabs hold of me and tells me to cut it out.

'Shut up, mate. It's a wicket.'

Kev comes over to me.

'Mate, you've got a chance for a five-fer in the Ashes.'

It's just what I need to hear. It gets my head back in the game.

This Australian line-up bats deep. Brett Lee, who is a dangerous striker and hits it miles, comes in. I bowl fifteen deliveries to him. He scores from none of them. I'm bang on line, bang on length, reversing it at pace. He doesn't like being tied down. He has only scored one. He goes at the next with hard hands, and nicks it to Tres, who swallows a sharp, diving catch, the ball as ever smacking straight into the middle of his palm. That guy's hand-eye co-ordination is unreal.

My first Ashes five-fer.

I trot back down to fine leg. I'm scanning the crowd, looking for the gobby Australian. All of the English fans are cheering and laughing. They know that I'm searching for him.

'He's gone to find a bit of rope,' one of them says.

It feels great, but I want six now. Gillespie's been in for what seems like hours. He's faced more than a hundred deliveries, which is a good effort.[7] Then he steps across and whacks me for six over midwicket.

'Bollocks, Si!' I scream.

---

[7] Gillespie was to play just twice more for Australia, but his final Test innings, against Bangladesh at Chittagong in April 2006, was one of the most remarkable in the history of the game. Going in as nightwatchman at number three, Dizzy batted for nine and a half hours, making 201 not out. His previous highest score had been 54. It's a great quiz question: 'Who was dropped after making a double hundred in a Test match?'

Vaughan immediately takes the new ball, even though it's the middle of my over. He knows I prefer the old one as it's reversing, so my thought is that he's planning to take me off.

So Gillespie's going to get it here, in the next four balls. He defends one, then another. The third is quick and straight and decks back in, striking him on the back pad. It would certainly have knocked out off stump, but he might have got outside the line too. We go up in a loud chorus. Gilly does his best to keep walking forwards and make it look as though he was definitely outside off stump.

When Steve Bucknor's under pressure he has this habit of licking his lips. He's licking them now as we roar at him. He knows it's close, but finally, finally, he nods his head and says, 'That's out,' as he raises his finger.

In the scorebook it says 'SP Jones 17.5-6-53-6'[8] but it means a whole lot more than that to me.

My first Ashes five-fer.

My Test-best bowling figures.

At last it feels as though I'm really at this party.

They say that you can judge the health of a team by its performance in the field. Today the long, long Old Trafford afternoon offers no comforting diagnosis. Australia look sick. Australia look tired and battleworn. They wear their scars on

---

[8] My figures were also the best by a Glamorgan bowler in Test cricket, beating the 6-118 taken by my dad against Australia in Adelaide in 1965-6. The record remains in the family, and I like to let him know about it.

the outside. McGrath and Lee injured. Gillespie forlorn. Warne and Ponting at war.

The England second innings starts in the same way that the first did, with Brett Lee hitting Andrew Strauss with a rapid bouncer, this one striking the grille of the helmet hard. His ear has been cut open. He feels the trickling blood. He pulls the helmet off. The physio runs out and sticks a big white plaster over his whole ear. Strauss pulls the helmet back on. He keeps going.

With just a few minutes to go before lunch Lee has no need to hold back, and he doesn't. Strauss edges a rising ball at catching height between first and second slip. Warne and Ponting both stand there and watch it sail past. Neither goes for it. Neither looks at the other. The crowd cheer. There's some shocked laughter behind me in the dressing room. Jeez. You don't see Australia do that very often.

We make it to lunch. Both sides know what's coming after the break. There are five sessions left in this match. The rain of the first two days mean that an extra eight overs will be available today and tomorrow. We must get far enough ahead that Australia cannot win, and we must do it quickly enough to allow time to bowl them out.

The lead is now 167. If Australia batted well for a day and scored quickly, they may make 350 runs, give or take twenty either way. That means we need another 200, plus a margin of safety – say fifty more on top.

This is the basic equation. Into it come other factors. The weather. The fifth-day pitch. The physical demands on the bowlers. The number we need will slide up or down on these scales. Seventy-seven overs remain today. There are ninety-eight scheduled for tomorrow. A total of 175 remaining in the game, minus two for the change of innings. If we score at about four runs per over it'll take around sixty-five overs to get another 250-odd, leaving Australia to chase about 420 with 110 overs available to bowl them out. No team has ever scored that many to win a Test, so if we can get there, we will be holding all the cards.

It's Tres who leads the charge, who strikes at their heart. He batters Lee's first ball to the cover boundary. He smacks his third through midwicket for another. An over later, Strauss uppercuts him over point for four. Tres clips McGrath through midwicket for four more. He cuts Lee to third man for another.

This is about more than just the run rate. It's about establishing a rhythm. It's about taking control. It's about letting Australia know what is coming.

Warne comes on to replace Lee. Trescothick whacks his first ball through square leg for four. Then McGrath gets lucky when Tres's straightforward defensive block hits the ground hard, rolls backwards and clips the stumps hard enough to dislodge a bail. Tres is gone for 41.

Vaughan goes in and hits Warne for four. He edges another through third man, where Gillespie fumbles, but he struggles for the form he had in the first innings and goes soon afterwards when he top-edges his favourite pull-shot off Brett Lee and Brad Hodge, who's on as sub, sprints around and holds a fine catch.

Bell goes in. Strauss ticks it along while Belly gets used to life out there. Bell walks down the wicket to Warne and misses. Gilchrist fumbles the stumping. Lee aims another rapid short one at Straussy's helmet. Strauss pulls him into the stands.

The hundred is up. Warne has one more over before tea. Strauss sweeps him for four to pass fifty and then bullies him for another. The lead is 270, and after the break it is only going one way.

Bell has played carefully since the Gilchrist miss, but when Ponting brings McGrath back, he climbs into him. He hits him back over his head for six, then drives him for consecutive boundaries.

Straussy smells a hundred and cuts loose too. He pulls Warne for six to enter the nineties and an over later pulls McGrath for four. His first Ashes century. Our second of the match. Australia are wilting under this assault. Ponting has his two best bowlers on and they're being picked off.

Strauss pulls off his helmet to salute the crowd. He's still got the white plaster covering his ear. It must have stopped bleeding by now. He's grinning and throwing his bat around. He'll get some stick for the ear later, but what a player.

He's a massive Jazzer, the poshest bloke in the team, public school, degree, all of that.[9] His nickname is Lord Brocket, after the Old Etonian peer who appeared on *I'm A Celebrity...Get Me Out Of Here*. Underneath it, though, he is a hard man. You have to be, physically and mentally, to open the batting in Test

---

[9] Strauss attended Radley College and gained a degree in economics from Durham University. 'Jazzer' is a semi-affectionate and widespread cricket term, short for 'jazz-hatter', referring to those hats they wear at public school.

cricket. Straussy is so strong mentally. Opening with Tres can be hard because Marcus has so much ability that he will go out and start belting the bowlers everywhere before mortals have got their eye in.

Strauss doesn't let what happens at the other end change his game. Cricket at this level is about self-knowledge. It's about understanding what you can do and accepting what you can't. Strauss knows his game, knows his shots, knows where and how he can score. He can be frustrating to bowl to because he's a brilliant judge of line. It often looks as if he's played and missed, but really he is playing inside the ball. His temperament is a little like Vaughan's. He'll be captain one day. I've only seen him lose his rag once, and that was with me. I bowled a very rapid spell at him in the nets in South Africa and got it reversing. He couldn't put a bat on it. He stormed out of the net. He told Fletch it was 'shit practice'. It was funny at the time, but then I realised that he was actually furious with himself. I related to that. He has that perfectionist streak, like me. He has the anger that comes from fear – fear of letting yourself down; fear of failing.

It's great to see him cut loose today. He showed his power as well as his control. He reinvented his technique against Shane Warne, taking an off-stump guard. He won the battle. When he mistimes another pull from McGrath and Damien Martyn holds the catch, he returns to genuine delight in the dressing room, delight for him, delight for us.

McGrath is special though, and he keeps on proving it. Injured, down on pace, assaulted by Strauss and Bell, he digs in. He fights. He gets KP first ball, leg before. He bowls Flintoff soon afterwards. Then he has Bell caught in the deep.

McGrath has five, but they have cost him a hundred runs, and another twenty overs on that battered body.

Warne has held an end, gone at three per over for twenty-five overs, but he has not taken a wicket.

Gillespie has bowled just four of the sixty overs so far. Ponting can't trust him, can't expose him. For an Australian great, a man with 250 Test wickets, it must be devastating.

Brett Lee has bowled rapidly but his twelve overs have cost sixty runs.

The ground fielding has been ragged. Gilchrist missed a second stumping. Australia are more vulnerable than they have been in eighteen years.

Vaughany tells us to get ready. The declaration is imminent. We want to have a short go at them tonight before the onslaught proper begins tomorrow.

Geraint gets the nod. He hits McGrath for a huge six over midwicket. He top-edges the next for a one-bounce four. He walks across his stumps to hit another miles into the stands. Vaughan doesn't even wait for McGrath to finish the over, doesn't allow him the chance.

Australia will need 423, more runs than any team has ever scored to win a Test match.

At the end of a terrible day for them, Australia get one slice of luck. The light goes. The umpires tell Vaughan it's good enough to stay on only if the spinners bowl, so it's Gilo and the skipper who bowl the final seven overs, and Hayden and Langer return to the Pavilion intact.

After play, Gilchrist goes on television to deny the Ponting-Warne story. Glenn McGrath tells a press conference, 'I think it's quite funny. I've been around the changing rooms the whole time and I haven't heard or seen anything like that. It's disappointing that it's in the papers when it never happened...'

England second innings 280-6 dec, Strauss 106, Bell 65; McGrath 5-115; Australia 24-0. England lead by 398 runs.

Day five

Ten thousand people are locked out of Old Trafford before the final day's play can begin.[10] Another ten thousand are told by police not to leave the city centre. Radio stations repeat warnings not to travel. The roads are gridlocked by 9 a.m. I arrive early and watch the huge queues swell and swell. Fred has a look and says, 'Mate, they're going to turn away a load here.' Harmi leaves it too late, and needs a police escort to get here before start of play.

The Australians come out and look too. They begin to understand what it is they will be facing today. The crowds have come to see us win. They have come to see them lose. This is special. We feel it as soon as we go out to warm up. They are already singing. They sound like people who have blagged

---

[10] Nineteen thousand tickets were available for the last day of the match, at £10 each for adults, £5 for children. The ticket office opened at 6 a.m., and the ground was sold out before eight. Lancashire's long-serving chief exec and former player Jim Cumbes said, 'You would probably have to go back to the days of Denis Compton and Don Bradman to see anything like it.'

the day off work. We are all part of something; exactly what we don't yet know.

I go through the usual mental checklist on how I want to bowl. I visualise taking early wickets. I prepare the ankle thoroughly. I try to keep a lid on the excitement but it's hard, especially when Hoggy is bleating like a sheep in my ear again. We end up wrestling on the outfield, the crowd cheering us on . . . Fred is pumped in front of his home fans. I wouldn't want to be facing him today, wouldn't want to be facing us. Vaughan calls us together.

'Lads, all we need to do today is exactly what we've done all series. Let's play our cricket the right way. Don't do anything different out there.'

It will be hard for Australia to resist it all: us, the crowd, the country, the collective will.

It will be hard, and for Justin Langer it will be impossible. He nicks the first ball that he faces from Matthew Hoggard and Geraint holds the catch. One gone already and in comes the captain of Australia, his team ragged, on the ropes, facing this group of bowlers that keep dismissing him, this crowd that is willing him to lose, willing him to fail.

These are the immediate pressures on Ricky Ponting but there are others too, pressures that come with being the captain of Australia, a job that ranks just under Prime Minister in terms of national importance. In Ponting's lifetime, Australia have been led by giants: Border, Taylor, Waugh. Men who didn't lose. Men who never yielded. Ponting has won too, won lots, won plenty, but now he must do the other part of his job. He must lead.

To me, bowling is the hardest job in cricket, but I see how batsmen sometimes stand alone. Ponting faces up. His body language sends a message to us, to his team: he's up for this.

Hoggy bowls brilliantly to him, bloody brilliantly, making everything awkward, putting the ball exactly where Ponting doesn't want it, lifting from a length, moving him across the crease with a fourth-stump line, letting him worry about the ball that comes back. Yet when Hoggy strays an instant from the perfect length, Ponting nails a drive past me at mid-on. When he leaves, he leaves purposefully, his bat held high above his head, his body close to the ball.

Hoggy has a good leg-before shout against him early, but Billy Bowden says no. Flintoff comes pounding in and over-steps. Ponting pulls him for six. The ball rockets from his bat. Haydos edges three streaky boundaries through the slip and third-man area.

They get to drinks. There are a couple of those Red Bulls in the drinks carrier as part of Fred and KPs sponsorship. The lads say they're good so I try one. It buzzes me up.

Gilo has a go. Hayden walks down the pitch and lofts him for six over long-off. Fred is bowling a ferocious spell, urged on by his people. Ponting plays it magnificently. He keeps out a spearing yorker. He gets right behind some fierce rising deliveries. When he gets on strike to Gilo, he rocks back and cuts another boundary. He wears a lifting ball in the meat of his chest.

It's exhilarating to be out here. I know I'll bowl soon, but Fred and I share an end, and he's not ready to hand over the ball yet.

He gets Haydos on strike. He goes over the wicket, with four slips. He pushes the first three across Hayden. Up close, the physicality of his bowling is extraordinary. He runs in with short pigeon steps before leaping at the crease and pounding his front knee down as a brace for his big shoulders to create the pace and bounce that he generates. The impression is not of grace but of unrestrained power. Haydos is just as big, just as aggressive, but Flintoff has dragged him across his wicket. The next ball is amazing, darting behind Hayden's pads and plucking out leg stump. The crowd goes absolutely nuts. Haydos squints down at the wreckage of stumps and walks off, out in the thirties again – 36 this time.

I bowl a couple of overs before lunch and feel sharp, but Ponting and Martyn make it through. Australia 118-2.

We know what we want, know what we need, but after lunch, with the overs ticking down it will not come.

The ankle burns. The ankle bites. Bone in flesh, flesh protesting. 'Fuck it,' I think, 'ignore it,' and from the Stretford End I find a nice rhythm. Ponting comes on strike. He's batting more easily now, any nerves gone, his eye keen, his mind sharp. I know I can trouble him though. The first innings dismissal gives me confidence, fires me. He defends a couple then I hit the perfect line, just on the stumps with a hint of reverse and he plays across it and the leading edge flies through a gap in the slips. The next delivery sinks into his pad and we have a big shout, but the ball is going down. The next reverses back at the stumps from very wide. He plays no shot and the ball takes his pad. We all go up again. Billy says not out.

We need something here, anything really, and maybe because those three deliveries have disturbed the post-lunch calm, maybe because Steve Harmison is pushing just as hard at the other end, maybe because we've kept the pressure on the umpires with our appealing, the gods smile down. Martyn is trapped bang in front and Steve Bucknor does a bit of lip-licking and gives it, and Martyn is already back in the Pavilion by the time the big-screen replays show the inside edge that deflected the ball into his pads.[11]

We don't care about that though, couldn't care less because an end is open. Six overs later, Fred has Katich caught by Gilo. In comes his bunny Gilchrist and Fred quickly knocks him over too, going around the wicket and reversing it away from the bat, drawing a thick edge to gully.

The game is swinging wildly: periods of calm accumulation that edge Australia towards safety; a little sunburst of wickets that keeps us striving, keeps us hoping. Drinks come: more Red Bull. Vaughan bowls a few overs to ease the burden. Tea arrives with Australia at 212-5, Ponting still there nine short of a hundred, one end open and forty-two overs still to bowl, forty-two overs that will shade this series our way or theirs.

Gilo and Harmi start. Ponting drives Harmi to the cover boundary to bring up his century. Now Australia have got one too. Now their captain has a hundred, just like ours. He pulls off his helmet. His hair is glued to his head. His face is pale

---

[11] Although TV replays were available to viewers and the crowd via the big screen, Umpire's DRS was not used in the 2005 series. It was introduced into Test cricket in 2008. TV replays were available to the third umpire for disputed catches and run-out decisions, though.

and lined. He salutes the Australian dressing room, but shows no joy, no pleasure. All of the hardships of the innings and the match are there instead. What a player he is.

This ground is a place of work today, a place of struggle. The crowd are hushed by it, drawn into the fight. Clarke is in with Ponting and playing nicely, despite his back. I keep looking at Vaughan and thinking, 'Come on, give me the ball, give me the ball...'

Finally he does. I ignore the biting and barking of my ankle. I feel the caffeine buzz of the Red Bull. I take a look at the ball. It's in perfect shape, thanks to Tres, rough on one side, like satin on the other, the colours almost indistinguishable.

Clarke knows I fancy him LBW, so I decide to bluff. I start bowling away swingers, one after the other, enough to get him into a groove of either driving or leaving. I feel him getting comfortable with the shape and the line. He's not shuffling on the crease like he was in the first innings. He's playing smoothly, feeling good. I keep bowling them.

A new over begins. Another away swinger another leave.

I walk to the end of my mark. The crowd are still quiet, too quiet. I gesture to them to make some noise and they respond right away, a roar that grows louder and louder as I approach the crease. I let the ball go, and I know in that split second that it's perfect, just perfect, on the same line as all of the others, but crucially, *vitally*, with the rough half of the ball where the smooth half has been, swapped around without Michael Clarke seeing or knowing, and before it is even halfway to him he has his hands high and his wrists cocked, ready to watch it shape away from the stumps and into Jonah's gloves like all the others.

He sees too late that it isn't moving away at all, it's moving in...and in that moment he says, 'Oh no,' loudly enough for me to hear, and then the ball clatters into the top of his off stump, knocking it out of the ground with a 'clunk' that sounds like music. The noise in Old Trafford is massive. The lads are charging at me, alive with joy. I turn around to the crowd behind me and salute them. The moment is perfect, one I'll always remember.

That's it now, surely that's fucking it. Surely Australia are broken by this assault. One over later, Hoggy pins Jason Gillespie in front of the stumps.

Now that's it, now they're fucked. Seven down for 264 and twenty overs to play...But Ponting refuses to accept it, refuses to fail. He glides me to fine leg for four and then pumps another down the ground. Warne carves a couple more. I come off. Hoggard comes off. Gilo comes on. Harmi comes on.

We strive...We strive and we work, and they resist. Ponting and Warne, not arguing now, at war with us and not themselves.

Harmi comes off. Fred comes on. Gilo continues. The overs tick down. The crowd grow louder, beerier. Ponting has been batting for six hours. They add forty, fifty, fifty-five...

Fred comes off. I come back.

Fuck the ankle, fuck the pain, just bowl...

Warne clips me for four through midwicket. He tries the same shot again and hits it in the air. Kev dives and gets both hands to it, but the chance is gone. Ponting cracks me behind square for four and slides another off his pads. Fourteen overs left. Gilo comes off. Flintoff comes on. We bowl. We work. They bat. They score. Warne hits a boundary. Two more overs drift by. Ponting drives me for a couple to reach 150. For a second he doesn't even realise what his score is. Nothing matters to him except staying there. Nothing matters to us but getting him out.

From the end he hates, Flintoff summons something from somewhere. His pace cranks up another notch. Warne spars at one and misses. He spars at the next and edges. The ball screams towards Straussy at second slip, but the extra pace seems to catch him out and the ball hits his knee and bounces up...bounces up and drops slowly towards the ground as somehow Geraint twists his body around and catches the rebound about an inch from the turf.

The adrenaline rush is huge. The whole place seems alive. Ponting's head drops. Warne trudges off. Eight overs to go. Two wickets to get.

Flintoff bowls a maiden to Ponting.

Tres chucks me the ball, but something weird happens as I try to walk back to my mark, something strange. My whole leg tightens, the muscle screaming, pulling my heel up towards my backside. I almost collapse. I signal to Vaughan. A physio gets me off. Harmi takes my place.

Nigel Stockill gets me to the dressing room.

'What is it, Nige?'

'Cramp.'

'What do you mean cramp? I've never had cramp in my life.'

'What have you been drinking?'

'Nothing...just that Red Bull.'

'Jonah, there's caffeine in them. You're dehydrated.'

Jesus. I can't believe it. I'm raw with myself. Nigel gives me fluids and tries to loosen it off, but there are only five overs left, no time for me to get back out.

I sit down and watch Fred come in. It's a Herculean effort from him in front of his own fans. His heart is huge, but so is Ponting's.

Ponting resists. Lee faces up to Harmi. He gets a single. Ponting flicks a boundary through midwicket. Harmi bangs one into this fifth-day wicket and it bounces hard and high at Ponting's ribs. He darts inside the line and flicks at the ball as it passes. The deflection from his glove is slight but just enough for Billy Bowden to see, just enough to have Billy Bowden lifting that famous finger to the sky.

Ponting slumps forward. He looks like an old man, all of the energy sucked from him. He drags himself off, barely noticing that twenty-three thousand people are standing to him.

Four overs remain. Two from Flintoff. Two from Harmison. Lee and McGrath at the crease. Twenty-four deliveries. One wicket needed.

The Australian dressing room beneath ours is so quiet I hear Ponting walk in, studs clacking. He comes outside to watch. Neither of us can do anything about it now. Flintoff bowls to Lee. Lee has a swish at one, but the appeal is turned down. Flintoff keeps him on strike to give Harmison a whole over at McGrath.

Three overs left.

Harmi gives McGrath the bouncer-yorker combination. McGrath avoids the bouncer and digs out the yorker. The ball almost rolls onto his stumps. He keeps two more out. He gets bat on another yorker, which goes to fine leg for four.

Two overs left.

I curse and sweat. I should be out there. I'm a fucking idiot for not being. I could take this wicket, I know it. I have just the ball for Glenn McGrath, just the ball for Brett Lee.

Instead I watch Fred bowl another majestic over that Lee somehow keeps out. There is one huge shout for a leg-before and I hope, we all hope ... but nothing.

One over to go. Stuart McGill runs onto the ground to tell McGrath something. God know what, at this stage.

McGrath leaves the first and misses the second.

McGrath dabs a single from the third and gets off strike.

Lee leaves the fourth and leaves the fifth.

One ball left. Shit or bust.

The crowd roar. Harmi strives. England watches, on televisions in houses and pubs and offices ...

The nation watches as Harmi tries for a yorker and gets it just too full, and Brett Lee clips it through the on-side field and raises his hands in the air, as jubilant now as he was crushed at Edgbaston.

This match. This game.

This game and what it does to us.

Beneath me I hear the Australians going nuts on their balcony: the mighty Australians, celebrating a draw against the team they have crushed for eighteen years. I'm not on the field to be in the huddle that Michael Vaughan calls.

'Lads, look at that balcony,' he tells them. 'They're celebrating like they've just won the Ashes. Remember this ... '

*

We sit for a while, drained by it all. When the crowd has gone and the ground is quiet we go down the stairs to the Australian rooms. I take a beer, see Ricky Ponting. He's got the colour back in his face now. He has batted for almost seven hours to save his country. I walk over and shake his hand.

'Immense,' I say.

'Thanks, mate. You weren't too bad yourself.'

I raise a smile, despite the tiredness and the sadness of not winning (so different from the sadness of losing).

We stay for half an hour or so, no one really able to let the game go quite yet. 'Bloody hell,' someone says. 'That was the best Test match for at least a week,' and the players of both sides laugh.

6. Injury

'*Get up, you weak Pommie bastard.*'

7 November 2002, Australia versus England, Brisbane.

I see his face as I lie on the stretcher. See his face and never forget it, a face burned into my mind. Pissed … leering … gloating. He pulls back his arm and throws a half-full beer can at me. It flies a few inches past my head. Steve Harmison is helping to carry me off the Gabba. He looks ready to drop the stretcher and jump into the crowd after the man, but he doesn't. Jason Gillespie is helping to carry me off too. He shouts something at the guy, I don't hear what.

My right knee's gone, I know it. Match over, tour over, maybe worse than that. Over in an instant. I don't realise it yet, but my face is white with shock and pain. It had been a simple chase on the first day of the first Test, an easy run after a push down the ground from Ricky Ponting, me turning from my position at mid-on and catching up with the ball just inside that long Gabba boundary, sliding into the turf to scoop it back, and then not sliding any more, not sliding because my boot is digging into the sandy sub-surface and has the full weight of my moving body jammed into it, the feeling of being in a car as the brakes are slammed on followed by a THUNK and then nothing, nothing but the stillness of the earth beside me and the distant sound of people running and shouting.

I know it's serious right away. I know it's over right away. I punch the ground again and again, not in pain – the pain will come soon enough – but frustration and despair.

They stretcher me down the tunnel to a room somewhere, a cold, air-conditioned room where a chill comes over me and a surgeon arrives to start digging his fingers into the back of my knee.

'I'm sure it's your ACL,' he says, 'but I just want to check.'

Fingers digging in again, the pain bright and sharp.

'Yeah, it's the ACL. I'll just . . .'

The fingers in again, in the back of my knee until I snap, until I lose it.

'Right, mate, you've checked it. You know what it is, now don't touch me again or you'll be making friends with my fist . . .'

He doesn't touch me again, then or ever.

Outside, in the hot Queensland sun, the game goes on without me.

My first serious injury was a broken leg. I did it about a week after I'd signed my first professional contract with Glamorgan. I was sixteen and in my final year at Millfield. I had to finish school before I could take up the contract. For some reason I decided to play in a house rugby match. It was raining hard and the pitch was soaked. The game had almost finished when someone came clattering into me and I heard a sound like a shin pad being kicked. I wasn't wearing shin pads. I went down just as the teacher blew the final whistle and everyone ran off to get out of the rain. No one realised that I was still on the ground. By the time I got up, they were just dots in the distance. I couldn't put any weight on the leg, and so I had to hop to the school medical centre, which was nearly a mile from the top of the playing fields.

The nurse said, 'I think you've sprained it.'

'That isn't sprained,' I said.

She sent me for an X-ray that showed a clean break through the tibia and fibula of my left leg.

I think that's where my high tolerance of pain began.

When I phoned my dad to tell him what had happened he couldn't speak at all, not a single word. He just handed the phone to my mum.

Richard Ellison, the Millfield cricket coach, went spare too. He refused to talk to me for six weeks. I began to realise what a stupid risk I'd taken with a career that had not yet even begun.

The leg wasn't pinned, and it healed in eight weeks, but it didn't set quite straight. I was left with a bow in its lower half, and it was now slightly shorter than the other. It meant that I ran more on the outside of my foot than I had before, and that the shinbone pushed up into my knee differently.

For a right-arm fast bowler, the left knee is a vital piece of the anatomy. It remains braced while the ball is delivered. Eleven times bodyweight passes through it. I weigh ninety kilos. Nine hundred and ninety kilos, every single time. Every single ball over the course of a career.

I was to learn how each injury comes with a cost, not just immediately, when it must be treated and healed and rehabbed, but later, when the small changes and accommodations that its legacy demands begin to accrue. The body is a single organism and change in one part invariably causes change in another. Small parts of the broken bone settled around my ankle, which flared up in 2005. The bow changed the mechanics of my run. My left knee was operated on twice, in 2006 and 2008.

Cause and effect.

When I was eighteen and really rapid, I got a stress fracture in my right foot. I'd had some orthotic insoles made for bowling and one didn't quite fit correctly. Also, my body was still weak from its growth spurt. I'd grown so quickly that when my parents came to collect me from school at the end of term, my mum had walked straight past me. I was permanently, ravenously hungry. I ate nine Weetabix at breakfast, two lunches, two dinners and nine pieces of toast before bed. I loved the gym but I didn't know what I was doing. I'd bench as heavy as I could for ten reps. The same with squats.

It had turned me into a far more fearsome bowler, but until I learned to train properly, I was vulnerable. Glamorgan's pre-season work was still of the old school. We'd have a timed two-mile run up to a certain point and back. We did the beep test and then had nets, three hours in the morning, another three in the afternoon. That was it. I wasn't strong enough for that.

My foot kept swelling and I didn't know why. We played

Yorkshire at Cardiff towards the end of the season. I'd complained about my foot in the previous game and everyone told me I was fine. I knew there was something wrong. It hurt to touch it. Just after lunch in the match against Yorkshire I couldn't do my shoelaces up, my foot had swollen so much. I had tears of pain on my face. One foot looked like mine and the other looked like a fat guy's foot. I was sent back out. I could only bowl at 75 mph.

Matthew Maynard called me in. He tore into me, told me they weren't going to pay me. He said that there was nothing wrong with me.

I was sent for a scan that showed a huge stress fracture. I had to go to the end-of-season do in a plaster cast on crutches. Matty apologised to me when we were up on the stage together.

It was a hard lesson though. It hurt to be doubted. When you're young you don't always know the difference between the usual aches and pains of bowling and the other more dangerous sorts of pain.

I was already becoming acquainted.

A night out almost cost me my place in that fateful game at the Gabba. Our final warm-up before the first Test was against Queensland at Alan Border Field. The last day of that game was going to be batting practice for the lads. I'd bowled in two innings and was down to go in at number eleven. Rob Key had already been dismissed, so we decided to have a night out. Keysey was pals with Andrew Symonds because they played

Built for speed: the batsman's view
of me. The ball will be arriving at
the other end in 0.4 seconds. . .

With my primary school team. I'm on the far right of the back row. We went all the way to finals day at Edgbaston playing soft-ball cricket.

An early award. As a lad, I was short and skinny – but I still bowled fast.

Cricket at Millfield. I grew so quickly that mum didn't recognise me when she came to collect me at the end of term.

Leading Glamorgan off after taking my first five-wicket bag, against Sussex. I was extremely rapid with a ball in my hand – and just as unpredictable.

'Get up you weak Pommie bastard...' The grim faces of my England teammates tell the story of my injury at the Gabba in 2002. Not that one idiot in the crowd cared...

This is how it feels to take wickets for your country against the Old Enemy. I've just dismissed Michael Clarke on that unforgettable first day at Lord's.

Geraint Jones brings the Edgbaston Test to an end. . . along with my agony. I thought I'd dropped the Ashes when I spilled Kasper at third man.

The most famous image of the greatest series. Fred and Brett Lee, both warriors, sum up what it all means.

'Pel Araf, Fred. . .' Flintoff learns the Welsh for 'slower ball' as we combine for Michael Clarke's wicket in the first innings at Old Trafford.

A moment of history as Shane Warne takes his six hundredth Test wicket, Andrew Strauss at Old Trafford. Warne was simply magnificent in 2005.

The captain stands up: Michael Vaughan's ton at Old Trafford asserted his – and our – authority.

Written on my face: watching from the balcony at Trent Bridge, knowing in my heart that my series is over.

Ricky Ponting walks off after being run out by Gary Pratt at Old Trafford. I could hear him yelling at Fletch as he walked up the steps.

An innings fit to decide any series: Kev walks off the Oval after his 158 on the last afternoon of the 2005 Ashes.

Four years of work went into this moment: the sweet, sweet feeling of winning back the Urn.

One of the proudest days of my life. We receive our MBEs from Her Majesty the Queen.
And we were much better behaved than we had been at Number 10...

And we were worried that no one
would come: Trafalgar Square,
13 September 2005.

together at Kent, so we went to meet him. There aren't many bars in Brisbane that Symo doesn't know, and we must have visited most of them. We got back to the hotel about 4 a.m. The bus was due to leave for the ground at nine, so we made a deal that if I woke up before Rob, I'd knock him, and vice versa.

I didn't get a knock. I woke up at five to nine. I knocked Keysey. No answer. I kicked his door. Nothing. As I got into the reception area I could see the minibus leaving. I went into full panic mode. First Ashes tour and I've got drunk and missed the bus. My first thought was that my dad would be spewing with me. Then I thought of Duncan Fletcher and Nasser Hussain... Graeme Swann had missed the bus on a tour of South Africa and Fletch never picked him again. I ran outside and hailed a cab. The fare was twenty bucks but I threw all the money I had at him – ninety dollars. I got into the dressing room. Nasser was sitting in there on his own.

'Nas, mate, I'm so sorry. Hold my hands up, I went out last night and got blind drunk. I'm being brutally honest with you.'

He said, 'Did you get any action?'

'Well...yeah...'

'That's all right then. Look, you've admitted you've done wrong, that's fine by me. If you'd made something up, I'd have been spewing but just go and try to explain it to Duncan.'

Fletch was firing slip catches on the outfield. He was only thirty yards away, but it was the longest walk of my life. He looked at me and put his finger up – that meant 'wait'. He finished practice.

'Where have you been?'

149

'Look, Fletch, I'll tell you what I told Nas…I got carried away…I'll take any fine you give me, any punishment.'

He didn't say anything for a minute.

'All right, you've told me the truth, not some cock and bull rubbish. The fine is $50. But I'm disappointed, Simon…'

That cut right through me. I felt like an idiot.

As it was, he selected me for the Gabba, a fateful choice…

Australians even sledge you when you've just got one of them out. On that steamy first morning at the Gabba, Nasser Hussain had won the toss and chosen to put Australia in. It would become as infamous a decision as Ricky Ponting's at Edgbaston in 2005, but we started okay.[1] Caddick and Hoggard opened the bowling and troubled Hayden and Langer. I nicked Langer off in my second over.

'Congratulations, mate,' Haydos said out of the side of his mouth. 'You're the leading wicket-taker in the Ashes.'

Ponting came in and he and Hayden batted through until lunch. We came out afterwards and I fielded at mid-on, enjoying watching Caddick run in hard and looking forward to my next spell.

At Alan Border Field the outfield had been perfect. I'd slid around without any problem. We hadn't gone particularly hard in the fielding warm-ups at the Gabba because of the heat, so when Ponting clipped one past me I sprinted after

---

[1] Australia ended day one on 364-2, with Hayden on 186 not out and Ponting the other wicket to fall for 123. Hayden made another hundred in Australia's second innings and they won by 364 runs after we were bowled out for just 79 second time around. Australia went on to take the series 4–1, by which time I was well into my rehab.

it, not knowing that the outfield has a lot of sand under the turf which makes sliding almost impossible. I went down with my left knee beside the ball, and instead of it slipping along the surface of the grass it dug in hard and meant that my right leg, which was fully extended with the inside of the knee facing the ground was jarred to a halt, the knee hyperextending outwards and destroying the anterior cruciate ligament. The ACL stabilises the knee and stops it moving from side to side. My knee lay twisted and limp, the foot pointing out. I grabbed at it. People surrounded me. Once the pain kicked in I felt sick. I pulled my cap down over my face. The crowd groaned as the big screen showed the replays.

Once the doctor had examined me and I'd been taken to hospital for scans, I was told that the injury was repairable with surgery that could be done immediately in Australia, or back in England.

I knew that the lads would be moving on to Adelaide after the match and my family were half a world away, so I elected to go home. I had to wait a week to fly, then travelled on my own, in first class, and drank plenty to numb the pain. As we neared the UK, the stewardess asked if I'd like breakfast. I ordered a boiled egg that came quite raw and that I spilled all over my trousers. When I got through customs, my dad and my cousin Geraint were waiting. Geraint had tears in his eyes, but luckily the egg stains broke the mood.

'Si, what have you been doing on that plane?'

'Not what it looks like, mate,' I said, and I realised how good it felt to be back.

The decision to come home was even more fortuitous than I'd thought. My surgeon, Derek Bickerstaff, found a further injury to the post lateral corner of the knee that the scans in Australia couldn't have picked up. Derek had fixed so many ACLs that he knew a lot of surgeons missed the secondary damage. If that had gone untreated, my ACL would have ruptured again within a couple of matches.

As it was, I faced eighteen months of rehab. I didn't drink for a year because it inhibits healing. Erjan Mustafa, one of the physios at Glamorgan, took my recovery as a personal challenge. I moved in with him for a period to keep the intensity of the rehab high. Erj became my best friend. The weight fell off me because I wasn't training. I looked like a ghost. These were dark times. My financial position was precarious. I wasn't on a central contract and had I been forced to retire, my insurance payout would have been around £20,000 instead of the £500,000 a more comprehensively insured player would have received. The ECB paid my full tour fee and then it was Erj and me against the world. Maybe some people thought I wouldn't get back. I kept in mind what Derek Bickerstaff had told me: if I stayed patient and did the rehab, my right knee would be stronger than the left by the time it had healed.

Some of the pain was horrendous. I had to regain a full range of movement, so Erj would put me on my front, bend my knee up and lie on it. I had to fight the discomfort and the fear that the knee was going to pop again. I cycled endless miles on an exercise bike, ten minutes at a time. Erj would send me out for a walk or some water between sessions and then lower the seat when I wasn't looking, so that the range was increasing without me knowing.

I worked as hard as I ever had to get back. The day finally came in a second-team game at Cwmbran against Lancashire. I bowled as quickly as I can remember. There were 200 press men on the grass bank. I nearly hit Chris Schofield and Kyle Hogg with wild beamers. I broke Paul Horton's foot. I didn't really care.

It felt so good just to run in again.

I was on my way back. My relationship with pain returned to the everyday. I bowled some very quick spells on an Academy tour of India, and then I came again to international cricket in March 2004 for England's tour of the West Indies.

It began what were in retrospect my brief years in the sun, and it was as if the gods of the game, as fickle as ever, decided to reward me with the biggest wicket of them all as the first of my return.

The series began in Jamaica at Sabina Park, for so long one of the fastest tracks on earth. West Indies batted, and with the first ball of my third over, I found the edge of Brian Lara's bat and the ball disappeared into the bucket hands of Andrew Flintoff. I thought my head was going to explode.

That Test became known as Harmison's match. He destroyed West Indies' second innings with his most famous spell, taking 7-12 as we bowled them out for 47. We won the game by ten wickets, and the next in Port of Spain by seven wickets. There I took my first five-fer, knocking over a very decent top four of Gayle, Smith, Sarwan and Jacobs on the way. We hammered them again in Barbados, this time by eight wickets, and very probably would have had the clean sweep in the final Test at St John's in Antigua had the umpire, Daryl Hair, given Brian Lara out when he nicked off fourth ball to Steve Harmison. Instead Lara went on to make 400 and reclaim the World Record Test score from Matthew Hayden, who had surpassed Lara's previous best of 375 when making 380 against Zimbabwe 185 days before.

It was a remarkable feat to watch, although after two and half days of Lara batting between showers on a damp ground and flat track, the appeal of his brilliance had begun to wear thin. I've seen nothing like it before or since: he simply hit every ball where he wanted. Vaughan would move a fielder and so Lara immediately struck it where the guy had just been.[2] I got grumpier by the hour, especially with some of the crowd, who were flipping us off down on the boundaries. We'd just smashed them 3–0 after all. When we eventually got off the field Brian said to me he was glad that I hadn't been given the third new ball, which in the circumstances I took as a compliment.

I played a couple of Tests that summer, against New Zealand and West Indies, and then came the tour of South Africa on which I established myself in the bowling line-up that would surge through to the 2005 Ashes. I knew I had pace and old-ball skills, but once I had begun to win the confidence of Michael Vaughan with the newer ball as well, I felt established within

---

[2] Lara's 375 was also made against England on the same ground, St John's, a decade previously in 1994. Graham Thorpe played in both games, and, ironically, given his role in giving Lara not out on nought during his 400, Daryl Hair umpired on both occasions. I'm convinced to this day that Brian nicked it.

the side. We won the series 2–1, and it was a massive hurdle for us to clear. The series gave me fifteen wickets at 26.66 in the four games I played, and I was pleased to add Jacques Kallis, AB de Villiers and Hashim Amla to my list of top-notch scalps. I began to feel that the Gabba had happened for a reason. I had returned a much better bowler with greater control and variation.

Then came the summer of 2005, and after that my sunburst was over. I still find it hard to believe that I never played Test cricket again. Instead I stepped into my years of shadow.

The ankle that troubled me so much during that Ashes summer was a comparatively easy fix. After the pain and swelling died away, I had it cleaned out; the bone spurs were removed, and so was significant scar tissue that was compounding the impingement. It cost me the tour of Pakistan, but I was selected to go to India in March 2006. It was to prove a benighted tour in terms of injuries. Michael Vaughan flew home with a knee problem that would ultimately force him into retirement. Marcus Trescothick returned with the depression and psychological difficulties that were to so sadly rob him of his international career.

Fred took over as captain. The day before the first Test I was bowling to him in the nets at Nagpur when I jarred my knee in a deep foothold at the crease. It gave a great and sinister CLICK as it happened. I flew home the next day, and I went back to Derek Bickerstaff for an arthroscopy. He cleaned the joint out and told me that he couldn't find any significant damage. It seemed at the time to be just another unfortunate twist, in both senses of the word.

However, I knew it wasn't right. It kept feeling as though it needed to click again. I played through it at the start of the English season. The medics were fairly convinced it was okay, and it was uncomfortable rather than genuinely debilitating, just another notch or two on the pain register.

I was fielding for Glamorgan in a forty-over game against Ireland, messing around with it again, idly moving it from side to side, when finally it clicked.

'Ah,' I thought. 'That actually feels all right.'

I ran in to bowl the next over and when I put my weight on the leg, the pain pretty much exploded through it, hot and sickening. This was real pain once again – I was now a man who knew it when he felt it.

What had happened was that a flap of cartilage – the substance that cushions the bones of the joint – had developed and folded underneath the rest of the cartilage in my knee. Derek Bickerstaff wouldn't have been able to see it, but it kept moving and feeling as though it should click. When it finally did, the flap broke off and bone began rubbing against bone, with eleven times bodyweight providing the pressure.

I went to Colorado to see Richard Steadman, who had repaired the knees of many famous sports stars and who had pioneered a technique known as microfracture, where the bone of the knee was deliberately broken to cause tiny fissures that stimulated the development of new cartilage.

He described my cartilage as looking like a fried egg. The

'yolk' at the centre of the knee was still intact, but the 'white' was crumbling away. He operated in June 2006.

'I think you've probably got about another two years on the knee,' he said.

Things at Glamorgan got messy. I would get fit and then break down with niggles and swellings and strains. My contract was up, and I moved to Worcestershire for the 2008 season on a two-year deal. I loved it there, loved the coach, Steve Rhodes, loved the people, loved the cricket, but I tried too hard and I bowled too much, 130 overs one month, and I bowled quickly too. They needed me and I needed them, and it was no one's fault, but it took a toll on my body that I could no longer meet.

Even when the whispers began that I was on the verge of returning to the England side, injury and luck intervened. I made a thirty-man preliminary squad for the Champions Trophy. I felt I was in the frame for the Test side to play South Africa in July when the selectors overlooked me, and Harmi and Hoggy, in favour of Darren Pattinson, who appeared just once. I was called up to the Lions in August after forty-two wickets in nine Championship games and tweaked a hamstring, and then a week later, the cartilage was damaged again and the season was over.

It was now three years since I had played for England. It was two since Richard Steadman told me that I might only have two years left. I began to consider that I may never come back. I was thirty years old. I thought of my father, finished at twenty-six.

I gave an interview to a national newspaper with a writer that I knew. He asked me if I'd heard from the selectors or the ECB. I said I hadn't, which was true. I'd spoken to Kevin Shine, the national fast bowling coach a few times, but until the injury finished me for the season, I had been concentrating on Worcester. The piece came out. I read it in horror. It lambasted England. It implied that I felt I'd been shunned, made an outcast. A week later I got a letter in the post from Hugh Morris, Managing Director of the ECB. It tore into me.

I thought, 'I'm not having this.' I rang Hugh, and said I'd come and see him wherever he was. The meeting was frosty at first, but I told him that I'd always appreciated their support, and that all I'd said in the interview was that I hadn't heard from the selectors, which was true. I hadn't. He knew that the journalist in question liked to stir things up so we kind of sorted things out, but the episode just added to my sense of unease.

I had more surgery on the knee in the winter. The surgeon, Andrew Williams, told me that I had an 80 per cent chance of playing again. I took the pills, did the rehab, told myself that it would be okay, that if I gave it everything, I would have no regrets. I had a family to support, a lifestyle to maintain, a future that yawned like a black hole if there was no cricket in it.

I missed the start of the 2009 season with swelling and discomfort in the joint. In April, Andrew Williams performed more keyhole surgery to clean out the broken cartilage. In June I had more scans. Then I had fluid drained from the knee. Then I was told I'd miss the rest of the season, the season that hadn't yet begun, the last one on my contract. In July, Worcester released me.

I talked up my future. I told myself and the rest of the world that I would recover. My management found me a deal with

Hampshire for 2010. It was pay as you play. I took it anyway. I was desperate for something, and Hampshire were so good to me. In the gym at Worcester I'd got as strong as a bull and almost as big. I weighed 107 kilos. I looked like a rugby player. All I knew was that I should meet weakness with strength.

At Hampshire, however, I began work with Iain Brunnschweiler. He told me I needed to be strong but light. He altered my gym work, changed my diet, streamlined me and reduced the load that my knee had to bear. At every training session, and at every net, at every warm-up and every game, every ball I bowled was logged and counted. Brunnshy calculated where my 'Red Zone' was – the area in which my body was being pushed too far and would be injured. Somehow he got me out on the park.

I was still quick – bloody rapid sometimes, especially with the white ball. I bowled well in West Indies, where we went to play T20 cricket. I played when I could, because if I didn't there was no money. I was worrying myself sick every day. It was consuming me. Was this how I wanted to live? I was waking up in the morning and immediately reaching for my knee to see how much it had swollen during the night. If it had, I would try to hide it, smiling at everyone down at the nets and choking down the pain and fear as I bowled. Every Monday I would have to do deep knee bends on an incline board, where bone rubbed on bone through its thin web of cartilage. My life became a game of trying to kid myself and kid others.

In the middle of the 2011 season I went back to Glamorgan on loan. I had mixed feelings about leaving because I owed Hampshire and my great friend Rod Bransgrove so much, but it got me playing. When I was fit I was still good enough, and I took wickets and bowled fast with the white ball.

Yet the reality was that I had played just three championship matches since 2008. Glamorgan offered me a deal to play in all formats for the 2013 season. We had a brief and glorious swansong when we got to the final of the YB40 competition at Lord's. I was thirty-four years old, had been a professional for more than half my life, and this was my very first final. We lost to Notts, but I bowled okay and it seemed like an ending of sorts.

I announced that I would retire from all cricket except T20 at the end of the season. I had no real idea what else I would do, but I knew that it was over. I waited and waited for a contract offer, but none came.

As soon as I made the decision, I realised what carrying on had cost. For four years I felt as though I had gone through life with a face on, one that pretended my life was something other than it was. It took a toll. I snapped at fans who asked how I was, and they didn't deserve it. At the heart of that were the injuries I was trying to cheat, but ultimately the body cannot be lied to for ever. My mind carried me through those years, and my desire not to get to the age of forty and ask, 'What if?'

I know now that 'What if?' is a loaded question. My 'what ifs' are about where my life would be had I got out sooner and charted a new, clear path. Injury cast a dark shadow, and it's one that I'm only now beginning to step out of.

But hey, buddy from the crowd at Brisbane...I will never forget your face.

7. Trent Bridge

In which I have a brush with the law, run through the enemy
again, fall out with the captain and coach, and feel a
crunch that changes everything…

There are ten days between the end of the Old Trafford Test and the resumption of the series at Trent Bridge. I go back to Cardiff, meet up with my mates Chris Peacock and Richard Childs. I met Chris when I was rehabbing my knee. I had to go and live with Erj while he did his stuff, and Erj was living with Chris in Chris's house in Llandaff. We have a few beers – more than a few. We walk back to Chris's from the pub. When I'd lived there we used to play cricket on his driveway. We decide that we fancy a game. I find an old ODI ball and a bit of kit. The game takes place under lights – street lights. Chris bats first. I bowl off a couple of paces. The alcohol has numbed the ankle nicely and I'm feeling absolutely no pain. I let a few go. The ball thuds into the side of the house. Things get raucous. It's fun. I feel good, free.

Someone calls the cops, or at least the police arrive.

'What are you doing lads?'

'We're playing cricket.'

'We can see that. Don't you think it's time you went home?'

'We are home.'

'Well knock it off, will you? It's two in the morning and you're making a noise.'

One of the great things about Wales is that it's a rugby nation. If a union international was having a 2 a.m. game of touch rugby in the street, there would probably be a crowd, never mind the police. I've noticed that more people seem to recognise me in the city centre, but mostly I'm anonymous here. I've seen how it is for Tendulkar in India, for Warne in Australia – not that I'm on a level with them – and it suits me to have a normal life.

The cops take the bat and ball from us and drive off to the police station, which is about 500 yards away. Chris runs up there, promises to behave, gets them to give him back the bat and ball. The game resumes. I end up bowling a few more overs than Fletch would probably like.

The fun ends soon enough, along with the temporary escape of booze. Two days of it and I have my game head back on. I get serious, hit the gym, keep my ankle in shape with ice and rest and no alcohol. It's sore though. I speak to Kirk about getting another jab in it. He thinks the rest will sort it out. I'm on a breakfast of anti-inflammatories and whatever else he tells me to take. It's strictly by the book now. I'm down on myself about the Red Bull cramps at Old Trafford. I wasn't out there on the field when I should have been. I could have got McGrath or Lee out; the elusive magic ball could have been mine, but I wasn't there to give the skipper the option. It eats at me. It fuels me. There are ten more days of cricket in this series, and I will play them. Of those ten, we'll bowl on what, four? Maybe five? I'm pretty sure I can nurse the ankle through, take the pain for a few more days, be out there with this group of lads. I've done it before and I can do it again.

The group is a powerful motivation for me. The last two years have been building towards these moments. Everything we have done, we have done together. Everyone puts up their hand. Everyone does their share. Now is the time for us to draw on the collective strength.

I feel good when I get to Trent Bridge. Fletch gets us together in the team meeting and tells us that we played better cricket at Old Trafford than we had at Edgbaston. Australia may think that they have changed the momentum by avoiding defeat in Manchester, he says, but they have not.

He says, 'Lads, look at them. They're a broken unit. Ponting's getting angrier by the day. So is Langer. They're not a happy camp. Just go out there and enjoy it. Soak it up. This is our chance.'

The mechanics of their batting line-up has been smashed. The way they used to run – like clockwork – has gone. They are so used to us running through them that they're ruffled. When they practice, they're not raucous and loud any more.

Fletch is right. We may be disappointed by the draw in Manchester, but the real problems are all theirs, the real pain is all theirs...

The problems and the pain...

Matthew Hayden's highest score of the series is 36. Adam Gilchrist's highest score of the series is 49. The pair that bring destruction to either end of the batting line-up yet to make a half-century in the series.

Justin Langer has admitted that they are troubled by the reverse-swinging ball. Buchanan is scouring Australia for bowlers that can do it. They're obsessing over it, talking about it in the papers and on the television.

For the week that we have been resting, they have been playing – or they are supposed to have been. A game against Scotland is washed out. A two-day match against Northampton goes ahead. They get no hint of a contest there. Hayden, Clarke, and Katich make some cheap runs. Shaun Tait takes some wickets. Glenn McGrath complains of soreness in his elbow after bowling a bouncer. Justin Langer tells the press that Australia have been 'lacking intensity'.

As a strategist, Fletch knows how to break people down. Australia ask for some fast bowlers for their net practice. Fletch sends Mark Footitt, a nineteen-year-old who's on the staff at Notts. He bowls left arm over with some serious heat. He was chosen for England U19s during the winter and got injured, but he has just made his first-class debut, and knocked over Saurav Ganguly, India's captain. The Australians know nothing about him.

I see Kasper walking away from the net session. His eyes are wide. 'Jeez,' he says to me. 'How quick is that guy...'

Fletch's message is clear: all of our bowlers are hostile. All of our bowlers will come after you. No easy rides. We can see that they're getting flustered, that their preparation is poor.

Our Tuesday session is as tough as always. I go hard. I have to. The ankle holds up. Fletch comes over to me.

'I need you to be fit, Simon.'

'I am. Don't worry about me.'

He knows that I mean it. I'd never say I was fit if I didn't think I could make it through the game. It's no fun being a bowler down halfway through a Test match.

Two days before the game Australia announce that Jason Gillespie has been dropped. I feel for Dizzy but it's no surprise. He got cleaned out at Old Trafford; Ponting couldn't bowl him. In the series his three wickets have cost 300. The crowds have been on his back. He has been a fearsome cricketer, but, sentiment aside, it is a hard blow for us to land on them. We've just taken 251 Test wickets out of the team.

Shaun Tait will take his place. They talk up his pace: Tait hit Langer hard in the groin in the nets and they had a few words. In the two-day game at Northampton he hit Tim Roberts hard in the head, Roberts needed six stitches. He bowls spearing yorkers and nasty bouncers from a low, slingy action that makes the ball hard to pick up from the hand.

We're not bothered. He'll be nervous on debut. He's been known to bowl a lot of no-balls and a lot of loose deliveries.

Then McGrath complains again of soreness in his elbow. He travels from Nottingham to London for scans. Errol Alcott says he's confident he will play. Ponting says he's confident he'll play.

Yeah, so confident that he's been sent to London two days before the Test...

We relax while they sweat on their champion.

Day one

When Thursday comes, any thoughts Australia had about a change in momentum disappear.

McGrath fails a fitness test and does not play. Mike Kasprowicz takes his place. Matthew Hayden keeps his place. Shaun Tait makes his debut. England are unchanged. The Australian warm up is quiet.

I sense the doubt, sense the angst.

Ricky Ponting loses the toss. Michael Vaughan chooses to bat. The Trent Bridge pitch is rough and brown. The outfield is lush. It suits swing bowling – if you know how to bowl it here – but the wicket is also slow and flat, even for Brett Lee, even for Shaun Tait.

Tres and Straussy have a look for a few overs and realise that the only demons at Trent Bridge are here for Australia.

Lee is rapid but gun-barrel straight – no seam, no swing. Kasper is bang on the money, but with no pace, no zip. Ten overs go by with no hint of a chance, no hint of danger.

Ponting takes off Lee and brings on Tait.

Tait is tall and powerful, thick neck, bow legs, broad chest.

He runs in smoothly, but at the crease everything collapses. His back leg folds, his front leg splays wide as he pivots over his knee, shoulders low. His arm seems to come from around his back in a wide arc, slinging the ball flat and hard towards the batsman.

It's the antithesis of the textbook, with its insistence on a high arm and sideways turn, but there is more than one way to get it done. Tait is rapid. The action may take its toll on his body[1] but he lives up to his nickname of 'Wild Thing'. In his fourth over, he stops the speedgun at 93.6 mph. In his fifth, every delivery except his deliberate slower ball is over 90 mph.

The no-balls are present though, four in his first five overs, the no-ball and the nerves, and he goes for plenty: Tres cuts him for consecutive boundaries; Strauss pulls him smoothly through square leg. He concedes more than five runs per over. The no-balls are catching. In his eighth over, Kasper oversteps three times. It costs thirteen runs, and Ponting hooks him off.

Shane Warne comes on after barely an hour of the first morning, with England already on 74-0, the scoring rate over four runs per over. Ponting is seeking control, seeking the order that has existed for so long when he had Glenn McGrath and Jason Gillespie to exert his grip. It doesn't come though,

---

[1] Tait's Test career was stymied by serious elbow and shoulder injuries that restricted him to three matches in three years. He gave up first-class cricket entirely in 2009. His fifty-over career ended after the 2011 World Cup, but he continues to flourish in the T20 game, where four-over spells best suit his unique action. In 2010, he produced a 161.1 kph delivery (100.1 mph) against England at Lord's, the second-fastest ever recorded. Once you're fast, you stay fast.

not right away, as Tres launches Warne straight for six and Strauss creams him through cover for four. But there is magic in Warne: even on a flat pitch and a dead day, he summons something. Strauss bottom-edges a sweep hard onto his boot, from where it bounces up to Hayden at slip; it takes a TV replay to prove that the ball didn't strike the ground as well as Strauss's foot.

There are 105 runs on the board already though, and Vaughany carries on from where he left off at Old Trafford, smacking Warne's next ball for four.

Lee comes back in place of Tait and forces Tres to drag a wide, angled delivery into his stumps. He's halfway through his celebration when he sees the outstretched arm of Aleem Dar. The crowd's roar for the no-ball call is part happiness, part glee at Australia's misfortune. Lee hangs his head. Ponting looks at the sky. Lee runs in again, oversteps again. Tres pulls him hard to the fence. The crowd's roar is even louder.

In the last over before the interval, Vaughan straight drives Lee to the fence and cracks the final ball through point. It's as if he's saying, 'Look, nothing has changed for you. This is just like Edgbaston…just like Old Trafford.'

The Australians trudge off, under the pump once more. The Nottingham skies echo their mood. The rains come down. At the moment, it's the only thing that can stop us.

*

The rains allow just four overs in the afternoon session, four overs that Kasper begins with a no-ball, the nineteenth in twenty-eight overs bowled. One has cost them the wicket of Trescothick, just as another cost them the wicket of Vaughan at Old Trafford. It's a nasty symptom to have, usually indicative of a deeper malaise. After Lord's, as if from nowhere, Australia have been besieged. From the dressing room we watch the rain fall on the covers, and wait.

We don't play again until four o'clock. Trescothick and Vaughan go out, and Tres is back almost immediately, bowled by a sharp yorker from Shaun Tait. Tait is invigorated by it, high on the endorphin rush and he suddenly looks like the real deal. An over later, he rips out Bell with another full one, the catch taken by Gilchrist. The ball is, if not swinging, wobbling in the air and at Tait's pace that's all it takes, especially with batsmen who are not yet set.

Kev goes in. His eye is unbelievable. He strokes Tait's first ball for a couple as if it was a loosener.

Tait bowls a beamer. He apologises. Kev smacks the next one back past him – he doesn't bother returning the apology.

Tait is quick but Kev's quicker. The sky brightens, even though there's rain in the air. Tait overcooks an attempted yorker that Kev whips through midwicket, the ball travelling almost too fast to follow.

The light gets slightly worse, the drizzle slightly heavier. Kasper starts to swing it. He gets one between Kev's bat and pad but misses the stumps. Kev survives. He plays a big on-drive to another full ball and it goes at catchable height to Kasper's right. He grasses the chance. He slams his fist into the pitch.

Tait comes off. Lee comes on.

Kasper starts a new over to Vaughan, who cuts him straight to Hayden in the gully. Hayden drops it. Kasper swings one back in at Kev who pads up. Steve Bucknor turns down a huge appeal.

It's crazy, all-action cricket, symptomatic of the match and series. I can't remember playing in games that have so few calm passages of play. On the other side of drinks, Vaughan pings Lee through the covers. Kev whips Kasper through midwicket. Vaughan leg glances Lee for four more. We're four short of 200 now, with just forty-six overs bowled. Nothing – not rain, not swing, not the fall of wickets – seems to stop us from scoring.

Ponting needs something now, needs something badly. There is no McGrath to turn to. Warne has a stiff back and work ahead. Ponting does something from so far out of left field, I don't think any of us are prepared for it: he brings himself on to bowl.[2] Vaughan guides his third delivery into the gully and Kev charges towards him calling for a single. He's sent back and would have been run out had the throw hit, but Hayden misses.

For a little guy and a non-bowler, Ponting is quite quick, almost 80 mph. It's not much slower than McGrath was at Old Trafford when his ankle was hanging off. He's getting some swing too. He tries to tempt Kev into something stupid, but Kev is content to leave – for now.

Vaughany smokes Lee for a couple more boundaries to bring up his fifty. He's in prime form now, and such a lovely player to watch.

Ponting hooks Lee and goes back to Tait. He keeps himself on. Like most top players, Kev and Vaughany actually look

---

[2] Ponting's last Test wicket had come in 1999 against West Indies at Bridgetown, where he had Ridley Jacobs caught by Mark Waugh.

more comfortable against the full-time bowler. Ponting is smart enough to see it, smart enough to sense the discomfort, and with the second ball of his fifth over, he coaxes Vaughan to prod at a gentle outswinger and he thin-edges it through to Gilchrist.

What a bonus. What a fluke.[3]

Fred goes in and smears Ponting to the third-man boundary, but the skipper has done his damage and we know it. The rains come again and the umpires call it quits for the day.

England 229-4, Trescothick 65, Vaughan 58, Pietersen 33 not out; Tait 2-62, Ponting 1-9.

Day two

We feel as though we're ahead, just. Australia feel that a couple of quick wickets will change that. It's a picture that's as hazy as the weather.

Vaughany preaches his mantra: relax, enjoy it, express yourselves. He tells us to take a look at the Australians. No-balls. Dropped catches. Missed run-outs.

'Lads,' he says. 'They thought they were just going to turn up this summer and beat us again. They're not ready for this. We are.'

Vaughan is right and we know it.

---

[3] And Vaughany was to be Ponting's final Test wicket, much to Vaughany's embarassment. Ricky bowled just twelve more overs in his career. Vaughany, who bowls occasional off-spin, has a notable scalp among his six Test wickets – in 2002 he clean bowled Sachin Tendulkar, also at Trent Bridge. Anyone can take wickets there!

Fred and Kev walk back out. Fred's making his gladiator entrance, helmet tucked under his arm. They're both big lads, Fred six feet five, Kev six four, and they go out with purpose. The crowd buzz at the thought of the mayhem they can wreak. The Australians will be worried about that, and they're right to be. They're facing an England that they have not faced before. Kev has imposed himself on international cricket in a period of months, batting at the emotional pitch of a man desperate to have his say. Fred's journey has been far longer, and in its way more fraught. At nineteen he was called the new Botham. It's a cross that every English all-rounder since the great man has had to bear. To the unknowing world Fred was another amiable giant, lacking Beefy's brash absence of doubt, but possessed of the same power with the bat and speed with the ball. The persona that Fred presented to them – and still does – is only partly true. While his game seems carefree, he cares deeply about it. Cricket means an immense amount to him. He gets very nervous in the dressing room, but hides it behind jokes and giggles. The wisecracks are part of the shield that he puts up.

He has lived with the disappointments that have accompanied the unrealistic expectations of him. Injury has already robbed him of an Ashes series. He has shown the breadth of his talent – spectacularly struck hundreds, five-wicket hauls – but not always together, and not always consistently. At times he has been too eager to please. To live with that and the disappointments of his injuries is a burden.

But right here, right now, this summer, it's all coming together for the first time. Vaughan and Fletch make him feel at ease, tell him to play his way. Vaughan is always reinforcing it: 'Do what you do. If you get out for fuck all, we'll back you.' Kev gives him a licence too. For a long time Fred had the burden of being the lad who belts it miles, but now Kev's doing it as well. He has pushed Australia back. The pressure has been shared.

I always feel that Fred is at heart a bowling all-rounder, yet he draws his confidence from the bat. Edgbaston was huge for him. He proved to himself that he could hammer the best bowlers on the biggest stage. As soon as he had, he went out and produced that immortal over to dismiss Langer and Ponting. The moment at the conclusion of the game when he knelt down and embraced Brett Lee, acknowledging cricket's capacity for cruelty as well as joy, showed the real man beneath the hype. By the time he got to Old Trafford and his home crowd, he was already a hero.

Now he watches as Kev nonchalantly flicks the first ball after lunch for four. He pats a couple of big Warne leg-spinners back down the wicket, watching the ball right onto the bat. He sees Kev clatter Lee for another boundary, this time off the back foot. He survives a big leg before shout when a Warne leg break takes bat before pad. He watches as Lee induces Kev to nick behind to Gilchrist to leave us on 241-5 and the innings in the balance.

Geraint Jones goes in. Fred loves Geraint. He and Harmi are always looking out for him. They hate the stick that he takes – we all do. The Australians have been harsh on Geraint but he is making his mark: the catch to end the Edgbaston match; the miracle grab to hold on to Warne's edge at Old Trafford.

But then plenty of people can keep wicket. Fletch put him

in the side to provide explosive power in the late middle order, to make the kind of demoralising runs in which his opposite number Adam Gilchrist specialises.

Fred decides to take the pressure off while his little mate has a look at the pitch and the bowling and the light. He carves Lee over third man. He hits Warne inside out through cover. He hits him for a one-bounce four over long-off. The crowd love it, bloody love it, and so do we, because we're sticking to our plans, sticking to our strengths, doing it when it matters, with the game on the line.

Jonah joins in. Brett Lee oversteps again, and he drives him hard to the boundary. The power he has is at odds with his frame.

Warne digs in. He wraps those thick fingers around the old ball and rips in as hard as he can, ignoring the flat deck, the slow spin it has offered him so far. When he does that he produces huge leg-breaks that dip in at the right-hander and then spit away. He fizzes one past Jonah's bat, then another. He forces Flintoff to defend. He wants to build pressure, draw the big shot.

Lee comes off and Kasper comes on. He strives for control. He berates himself when he slips one down the legside that Fred glances for four. Despite that, he and Warne work together, dry up the boundaries. The new ball is eight overs away.... Then six...then four...

Warne errs first, bowling short and wide to Fred, who breaks the dry spell with a fierce cut. Three hundred draws nearer. Then Kasper drops short too, and Jonah belts him hard to the fence. Three hundred comes up. Fred sends the final delivery with the old ball flying over the square leg boundary to raise his fifty. There's a group of lads in the crowd where the ball ends up wearing shirts that spell out FREDDIE when they all stand up together.

The new ball comes.[4] Australian hopes are invested in it. We know the feeling. When nothing's happening and you need wickets, you yearn for it, you find yourself chewing through the last ten or fifteen overs of the old one, the captain trying to keep his front-line bowlers fresh for a new assault.

Yet the new ball can suit set batsmen just as well: harder off the bat, faster over the outfield. Tait gets first shot with it, and Jonah makes his mark. He smashes the first delivery through cover for four. A statement. A message.

Lee gets the other end, and Fred punches him for another. He gets on strike to Tait. He pulls the third ball of his next over hard and flat to the square-leg fence. Tait overcompensates and Fred drives him for four more. Tait bangs the final ball of the over in short and Fred has all day to pull him to the boundary again.

We love it, bloody love it. I can't remember the dressing room being this relaxed. Lads drink coffee, chat, look at magazines, but mostly sit down and watch and feel part of the whole thing.

This is Ponting's nightmare come true. Lunch arrives with the score at 344. He knows what is coming next. He doesn't need a crystal ball to see it. Another assault. More pain.

---

[4] In Test cricket the fielding side can take the second new ball at any point after eighty overs have been bowled (and get another after 160 overs, and so on).

The onslaught resumes immediately. Lee's first over of the afternoon costs nine. So does Kasper's. Lee's next goes for six. Kasper's next costs fourteen, studded with three boundaries that take Flintoff into the nineties.

Ponting has to do something. He turns to Warne, even though the ball is just thirteen overs old. Jonah walks down the pitch and smashes it back past Warnie. Jonah's fifty comes up. The 150 partnership comes up.

The 400 arrives in Warne's next over, when Fred flicks him for three. The crowd is alive, willing Flintoff towards a hundred. It's an electric moment. We gather on the balcony, ready for it.

He gets a single to go to 99. Jonah slaps Tait for four. Warne bowls a maiden to Flintoff. Tait bowls another to Jones. Warne gets Flintoff on strike again. He fiddles with the field, makes him wait. Ponting brings men in. He wants Fred to blow it, to panic, to hit over the top out of the rough, but Fred smiles and holds his nerve and works the ball into a gap to get that special, special Ashes hundred.

Trent Bridge has lift off. Fred is becoming a legend before our eyes.

Tait gets him with an inswinging yorker that hits him on the boot, but it's too little, too late for Australia. Gilo goes in. He hits Tait for a boundary and Kasper for two more. He sweeps Warne for another. Jonah nudges and runs, pings a boundary and then gets unlucky with his own hundred in sight. He drives hard at Kasper but the ball goes from bat onto pad and balloons. Kasper dives flat out to grab it.

Warne gets Gilo in the next over, then Harmi, who tries to heave him into next week, falls over and is stumped.

I'm in, and I'm going to enjoy it. Warne's doing his usual, just looking at me and laughing. We both know what he's going to do: throw it up and see if I'll take him on. He tried it at Old Trafford and bowled me for a duck. For some reason – and I don't know why because he's a genius – I like facing him. Maybe his genius is actually the reason. I can pick his googly too, not that he bowls it very often these days. He does throw one up and I take a swing and ping it over long-off for four. The next is flatter and quicker and I stick it through cover for four more.

Brett Lee is a lot less fun. He gives me three short ones to start with. Warne bowls a maiden to Hoggy, who doesn't seem to have any plans to swap ends.

Lee bowls me three more short ones. I'm pretty sure the next will be the yorker, but he double bluffs me and it's another in the ribcage. It smacks me hard in the chest, and goes down on to the stumps, but somehow the bails don't come off. I don't know whether to be pleased or not. Brett certainly isn't.

Hoggy cuts Warne for another boundary, but the fun's soon over. He feathers an edge to Gilchrist, and we walk off laughing with 477 on the board and Australia ragged, tired, the game to all intents and purposes beyond them already.

*

Bowling – and specifically bowling fast – is without question the hardest job in cricket, but I'm willing to concede that opening the batting is up there close. Hayden and Langer have been doing it for years and years, innings after innings, Test after

Test, marching back out into the guns against all attacks in all conditions. Days like this are the hardest of all, when the team has been kept in the field, and they never know quite when the moment will come, and they must be ready for it because the scoreboard is against them, and the crowd is against them, and they are tired and drained and the ball is new, and they know that if they fall then their team is opened up...

You must be mentally strong to resist, bloody-minded and determined, yet the grind can be relentless too. It is not just the position of this game that weighs on them, but the state of the series, the expectation and the hope, the doubts and the fears that have been growing and growing through a summer that has refused to bend to their will. It's making Langer angry and it's making Matty Hayden mortal. Until a year ago, he was the most feared opener in the world, a battering ram that drove through opposition attacks, destroying their morale and their figures long before the middle-order big guns had even had the chance to take guard. His average was over. But since then, nothing. No Test match century in twenty-eight innings. An average in that time of 31.

The whispers have started, and there is no doubt that he hears them, feels them. Some are suggesting that he had grown fat on poor bowling and slow pitches. Now the bowling has changed, but he hasn't. He still wants to drive the ball as soon as he goes in, still wants to play those meaty pulls and brutal cuts, still wants to get fifty on the board before anyone has really blinked.

We've worked hard on stopping him. We know the delivery that troubles him – Hoggy swinging it back into his middle-stump guard. We've had him caught at short cover, bowled and leg-before. He can't get beyond the thirties. In the first innings at Old Trafford, he batted so carefully it took him almost two hours to get 34, and then was done in the flight by Gilo. In the second innings he came out blasting, hit a big six and then got bowled behind his legs. No quarter either way.

Langer has always been his mate and his foil, his perfect counterpoint, nowhere near as spectacular but just as vital. By upsetting one half of the pair, we've managed to get at the other too. One of our aims is to make sure that they can't rotate the strike in the way that they like to, to give all of us time to work on them individually. So far it has worked, so far we have spread doubt and fear – not physical fear, but something more insidious: the fear of more failure, the fear of the end. Yes, bowling is hard, but that is hard too, and they know it as they walk out after tea to begin the Australian reply. They know that they must hold firm, or the game could be gone.

It takes nine overs for their nightmares to come again, for the doubts and the fears to become real. Hayden has made 7 from twenty-four deliveries. Langer has made 11 from thirty-two. Hoggy and I are bowling. My first over is a good, tight maiden to Hayden. Twice I go past his outside edge. The second is almost another – he pushes a single from the final ball. The ankle has been massaged and stretched, hyperextended and warmed up, dulled and drugged and it feels sore but tolerable – just. I'm ready for it now, the electric pain that runs up the outside of my foot and into the bottom of the leg, the burning of a raw nerve. It won't stop me, not yet.

Hoggard stops Hayden though. Big Buzz's nightmare is of the recurring kind. Hoggy takes the first ball of the tenth across him, and then brings the second back in. It sinks into his big front pad and we're up and shouting, yelling to the heavens, but Aleem Dar has seen the ball shave the inside edge of Hayden's bat, and this is what saves him. Hoggy simply runs in and bowls exactly the same ball again, Matthew Hayden plays exactly the same shot again – the nightmare, recurring – and this time there is no inside edge, this time there is just pad, and this time Aleem Dar's finger is up before the appeal is out of our throats.

Mayhem at Trent Bridge. Joy for us, joy for the crowd. We mob Hoggy. He's cracked them open once again. He brings Ricky Ponting to the crease long before he wanted to come. And every time he comes it must feel as though the Ashes are on the line. Perhaps they are.

You know the plans to a guy like Ponting. He knows that you know, and you know that he knows that you know. We both understand that sometimes they work and sometimes they don't. They are based on small chinks in the armour of a great player. What I try and do is execute those plans to the maximum of my ability. Quick, straight, top of off stump, and then bring one back, try to drag him across his stumps with a heavy head, leave him vulnerable to bowled or LBW while playing slightly across the line.

He knocks Hoggy for a single to get off the mark and I have him on strike right away. The first is bang on line, bang on length with a hint of shape. He pushes it to mid-off. The second is straighter – deliberately so – and he comes across the stumps and pushes into the leg side.

The third is perfect – bloody perfect – on the same line as the second but this time with enough inswing to duck past his bat and his heavy head and smack into his front pad as he walks at the ball.

Stone dead, third nut…

Steve Bucknor licks his lips. Steve Bucknor lifts his finger.

More mayhem in the crowd. Music to our ears. Ponting's world collapses inwards again.

Damien Martyn comes in and pushes me for a single. Hoggy gets him on strike. His first ball is magnificent, starting on the stumps and looking as though it will swing away before holding its line at the last. It thwacks into Martyn's pad and up we go again.

Aleem Dar gives it, and it's not until the big-screen replay comes that everyone in the ground realises that Martyn has got a thick edge on the ball.

That's the way it goes though. Sometimes you're lucky and sometimes you're not, and today it's us who are lucky. We've waited a long time for it.

The crowd, high on Flintoff's knock and the Australian disarray, are roaring as if they are at a football match.

Justin Langer digs in. Adversity always brings out his best. He drives me smoothly for four.

Clarke is in and I fancy him, but I know I'm coming towards the end of a spell. I get one more over after drinks, but again Langer is on strike, and again he drives me for four. Vaughany gives me a nod and a clap. I come off. Fred, to more cheers, comes on.

Hoggy's the man though, it's his day today, and he's got it

on a string to Langer and Clarke. Langer thick-edges a streaky drive through the gully for four. Clarke is beaten all ends up by a perfect, late-moving away-swinger, but the edge falls just short of slip. Hoggy's strength is amazing. He's through eight overs, then nine, then ten, all at good pace, all asking the right questions.

Flintoff goes short to Langer, who appears to lose sight of it. The ball ricochets from the grille of his helmet with a loud thump. That must have hurt, must have shaken him up, but it just jogs through for the leg bye.

Three deliveries later, it takes its toll. Langer pushes fretfully at a Hoggard inswinger and edges it into his pad. Belly holds a sharp catch at short leg.

Langer has fought for an hour and a half for 27, but it comes to nothing, it ends here.

A dreadful day for them. A wonderful day for us.

We push for one more, but Clarke and Katich edge towards safety, Clarke playing smoothly, Katich gutsing it out. Harmi gets the last over. It's rapid. Clarke thick edges the first over Flintoff's head at slip for four, defends the second and then plays all around the third, all around a ball that's doing nothing except knocking out the middle stump, and for the second time in the series, Clarke is dismissed by the last ball of the day.

Harmi looks like a wild man.

Perhaps we all do.

When I watch the TV highlights in my room, I see that Ponting got a nick on his leg before too.

*

England 477, Flintoff 102, GO Jones 85; Warne 4-102; Australia 99-5, Clarke 36; Hoggard 3-28. England lead by 378 runs.

Day three

I get out of bed and run through the ledger of aches and pain. I uncrumple myself, get down to breakfast, swallow the pills, head early to the ground.

My ankle is bad in warm-ups but I still think it's going to be okay. The general pattern is that it's electric and sore when I first start bowling on it, then it begins to ease. Vaughany wants to start with Hoggy, because he bowled so beautifully yesterday, and Fred, because Gilchrist is in.

I know I'll bowl first change, because we worked the wicket out yesterday. It responds best to the fuller length that Hoggy and I like.[5] Apparently Gilchrist has told the press that after Manchester, where he made 4 from thirty deliveries, he is going back to his natural style of playing freely whatever the game situation. After four overs he does. He wafts Hoggy over midwicket for four and then hits the next ball into the crowd beyond long-on. He takes a single, and then Katich pings the next two through point for four. Hoggy's over costs twenty-two. Vaughany rolls his shoulders at me. In Flintoff's next over, Katich smacks two more boundaries. In Hoggy's next, Gilchrist and Katich each take a boundary.

---

[5] My 'natural' length – the one I would bowl unless trying to do otherwise, was measured by Troy Cooley at six metres from the stumps. Hoggard's was similar, while the natural lengths of Flintoff and Harmison were eight metres from the stumps.

Hoggy comes off and I come on. Katich is on strike. I don't like bowling to him. I find him awkward. He's a leftie with a strange, square-on technique. He stays back in the crease, walks across his stumps and carves and drives into odd areas. I've spent a lot of time and wasted a lot of energy bowling at his pads for LBW, but he's very adept at clipping the ball off his legs. He never misses.

I decide to forget about the straight one. Instead I go across him, pushing the ball way outside off stump. Vaughan sets two gullies in a trap he fell for at Old Trafford.

My first ball flies harmlessly past off stump, but I barely see it. The pain from my ankle runs from my foot up into my calf and the back of my leg, worse than it's been before.

'Don't panic,' I think, 'it'll ease. It always does.'

I push the second one even wider of Katich, full and right out into the footmarks, and as if he's making an offering to alleviate my pain, he reaches out for it and plinks it straight to Strauss at the wider of the two gullies.

I'm feeling no pain now, no pain at all after that, as the adrenaline buzz shoots through me, more effective than any jab or pill I've ever taken.

Warne walks out at 157-6. He's become the patron saint of lost causes this summer. Now his back is against the wall once again. This time there's no way out. This time the well is dry. The ball I bowl him is quick and straight and it skids in at his pads. The late movement squares him up. The ball smacks into a leading edge and loops gently to Ian Bell at short cover.

Warne goes 'Ohhh' as he realises what has happened.

From nowhere, I'm on an Ashes hat-trick.

Brett Lee comes in. The crowd have woken up. The hairs on my arms have lifted.

Vaughan makes Lee wait. He arranges the field around him. He makes me wait too, though, and I start to overthink it. Brett likes to chase it but he might play and miss...Maybe I should go at the stumps.

In the end, I do neither and he defends it well.

Flintoff stays around the wicket to Gilchrist. He pounds the ball into the pitch, flogs some life out of it with sheer physical effort. Gilchrist goes for a little half-bat cut shot, but the ball gets big on him and flies hard into the empty air where third slip would be if we had one. From nowhere – well, from second slip, but it seems like nowhere because the ground he covers with his dive is so great – comes Andrew Strauss, who at first seems to go for the catch with two hands, and then, when he realises how far away from the ball he still is, throws out his left and plucks it.

It seems to happen in slow motion, even though the ball was travelling. As Gilchrist walks off, it's on the big screen and everyone, the crowd, the players, turn to watch the replay, which shows just how good the catch was. There's a great gasp and then sustained applause.

Great for Straussy. Great for Fletch, who drills us so hard in the field for moments like this.

Kasper comes out. He has a swing at Fred and edges four. He comes on strike against me. I bowl him an absolute peach that starts on leg stump and swings late and fast to knock out off.

That would have got many better batsmen than Kasper. He lets out an 'Ooooh' of shock and surprise as the ball goes past. I give him a smile. He doesn't smile back. I need the final wicket for my five. The ankle is killing now. When I run in to bowl, I'm splaying my foot to ease the impact, but it's affecting my gait and my action. I can feel it all deteriorating. The ball's not coming out as truly as it was. I try a couple of slower ones, but Lee belts the second for a huge six over long off. He heaves another over slip for four more.

I look at Vaughan. He keeps me on. Lee hits Harmi for another six, even further this time. I watch the ball get smaller and smaller as it goes over the stand and out of the ground.

I bite down and put up with the pain, but the ankle is crunching, which makes me feel as if I want to puke. I bang one in for Lee to chase and he obliges, carving it in a great high arc to third man. Belly trots around and bags the catch.

That's it. They're done. It's taken us 49.1 overs to wreck one of the great batting line-ups. They're miles behind here, absolutely miles, and there should be no way back. The captain calls a huddle on the field. Before he can speak, I do.

'Vaughany, I've got to go and see Kirk, my ankle's in bits.'

He nods. I run off the field as quickly as I can. I find Kirk by the massage table.

'Mate, I'm really struggling here. I'm walking like I shit myself.'

Kirk takes a quick look at it and says, 'I'll get a doctor up.'

As we wait, someone sticks their head in. 'We've made them follow on.'

'What?'

Jeez. That's what the huddle was about.

My first thought is, 'Oh God, what's Vaughany going to say now? Because I'm nowhere near right.'

The doctor comes in and jabs me with a local. The next ten minutes are a blur. The anaesthetic kicks in quickly, and by the time we're back out there, the whole foot is numb. Kirk could hit me with a hammer and I wouldn't feel it.

Hoggy opens up to Langer, who drives the second ball to the boundary. He flicks the final delivery off his pads towards me at long leg. I can't feel my foot as I jog around to collect it.

Vaughany asks me to open up at the other end. I've worked so hard for this, to gain his trust with the new ball, and all I can do is panic. Fuck it.

I get to my mark and run in. The best way to describe the feeling in my foot – or rather lack of it – is to compare it to the numb lip you get when the dentist injects Nembutal in it, except it's so numb that all I can sense is a kind of vague heaviness. When I plant it in the crease, I have no idea where it is, and it throws the rest of my action out. Something I could do in my sleep I now can't do awake.

Hayden somehow plays and misses at the first delivery, probably because it's so slow. It takes him a few more to realise that there's no pace and no swing, then he crunches a pull-shot well in front of square for four.

I bowl one more over before lunch and get off the field.

*

The afternoon quickly becomes nightmarish. I stay off for a while to see if any feeling returns. I'm beginning to think they've put too much anaesthetic in. I've been jabbed before and it hasn't felt this way.

Our fielding sub is Gary Pratt, a lad from Durham who plays in their second team but who is shit-hot in the field. It's one of Fletch's favourite tricks. It shows his attention to detail. From time immemorial, teams have just used whichever lads are available from the local county for twelfth-man duty. But Fletch likes the bowlers to get off the field after each spell, have a quick comfort break, put on a new shirt and go back out. While we're off, he wants a fielder who's been drilled as hard as we have.

Throughout the summer this has been winding Ponting and Buchanan up. It shows us that silly little things are starting to get to them.

Pratty comes off and I go out. They've got to 40 without loss. Hoggy gets clattered for a couple of boundaries by Hayden. Vaughany tells me to warm up.

I'm trying to get myself ready mentally when Fred does Hayden, moving one away that he hits to gully. I forget about the ankle for a minute.

Ponting comes in. I come on in place of Hoggy. It's the same woozy dread. It somehow doesn't feel real. I'm virtually jogging in and placing the ball. Langer senses it and drives me for four. I bowl one more over, to Ricky Ponting. I know I'm in his head, but he plays it easily. I call the captain over.

'Vaughany, I could break my leg here. I can't feel the ground when I'm running. There's no point me being here.'

He looks at me.

'All right.'

I go. I sit down in the quiet dressing room. It's as bad as I've ever felt at a cricket ground, worse than dropping the late chance at Edgbaston. I feel useless, as if I've let people down.

Kirk comes in. I tell him how bad the ankle feels. He says

that Ian Winson's at the ground and he's coming up. Ian is one of best orthopaedic surgeons in the country. He specialises in ankles.

I speak to Ian several times over the next hour or so. Fletch is buzzing between the massage table and the balcony, where he watches Ponting and Langer accelerate smoothly. I see him pulling Ian into another corner of the dressing room and questioning him. The second or third time it happens, it really starts to fuck me off. My head's starting to go. I feel like shit. I'm in pain, and Fletch is talking to the surgeon and not to me. I don't like being ignored.

He finally comes in. I lose my rag as he does.

'Fletch, I'm not in the mood for this. My ankle's in bits. I've had two cortisones this series. I've bowled in agony. Now you're coming at me with this. Why wouldn't I want to be out there?'

He says, 'It's not like that...'

'Well it *is* like that. You're over there with Ian...Chinese whispers, asking him how I'm feeling. Bring him over here and we'll talk about it.'

I know where the anger is coming from. Early in my career, the stress fracture that they didn't believe I had. Old doubts and old fears, but they're only buried, never gone.

I go and have a couple of cigarettes at the top of the Pavilion and try to calm down. My temper is the sort that builds and builds and then I blow, and I don't want to do it, with the lads out there fighting. It quietens down a bit. Kirk takes me to the hospital for a scan. They put the ankle in a boot. We get back to the ground just before tea. Some of the lads come and ask how I am. I hold the boot up. Fletch and Vaughan talk, but neither acknowledge me. I know they're busy, and it's the way of sport. Once someone's out of action and there's nothing you can do about it, you move on. Deal with what can be dealt with. Leave the rest.

But Vaughan may not have enforced the follow-on had he known I couldn't bowl. The other lads are fresh – none of us had had to work that hard in the first innings after all – but four must do the work of five now. Langer and Ponting are batting under extreme pressure,[6] but they are hardened players. They have calmed the crowd and subdued the bowlers and they are beginning to score freely.

Fletch and Kirk decide to leave me alone. I sit on my own and watch the game. Soon after tea, Gilo gets Langer, caught at short-leg by Belly. Martyn goes in.

Ponting is grinding it out, but he looks in no trouble. He knows that only another innings like Old Trafford can get them out of the shit that they're in, so he sets his stall out to play one. Once he's in, he's rock solid. He eases towards fifty. Martyn looks untroubled, but then he always looks untroubled.

Fred comes in to Martyn. He pushes to cover and calls for the single. Ponting goes right away, but it's a tight one. Martyn has hit it straight at the fielder, who happens to be Gary Pratt. Pratty's on it before Ponting's in full stride and he throws the stumps down with one flowing movement, arrowing the ball at a target four inches wide. Ponting lunges rather than dives and I can tell from the reaction of the lads that they think they've got him. Everyone turns to the big screen, every single soul in Trent

---

[6] Australia had not followed on in a Test match for seventeen years. It was probably not a record that Ponting wanted to break.

Bridge. Ponting realises at that moment that it's the sub fielder who has run him out. The replay shows him about a foot short as the bails come off.

The roar goes up and up, louder and louder. The crowd have these red cards with the word OUT printed on them by one of the sponsors, and as Ponting walks off there are about six thousand of them being waved at him.

As he walks up the Pavilion steps he pulls at the strap on his helmet and tries to make eye contact with our balcony. The rooms at Trent Bridge are on different levels, the home dressing room below the visitors, so he has to climb the steps and walk right past me.

He's yelling up at Fletch: 'You smug fucking ****…you fucking cheats, you're mocking the game…'

Fletch gives him a little smile. I realise Ponting is shouting about Pratty being on the field again. I don't give two shits that it's about me too. I think it's the moment he realises that they'll probably lose the Ashes. They're mentally exhausted, fighting battles they can no longer win.

Punter's barely shut the door behind him when Martyn follows him up, caught by Jonah off Fred.

Kirk brings the scan results back from the hospital. He says that the damage is about the same as it's been on the last couple. I feel as though I'm being accused of something. I know deep down that scans can't show the full picture. The anger bubbles up once more.

'It's bullshit that scan, Kirk. I don't have a reason to lie. I'm in agony here…'

He gives me some space. It's the best thing. I don't understand what's happening with the scan. I don't really care. I know this game's over for me. I know the series is gone. If there's one thing I understand, it's pain, and I know what this pain means.

Clarke and Katich bat out the remaining overs. My foot's so bad, Belly has to drive me back to the hotel because I can't depress the pedal in my car. I try to leave quietly, but the Australians see him helping me across the car park. I think that's when Ponting realises Pratt was on the field for a genuine injury.

I leave Belly at reception. I get myself upstairs. I order room service. I ignore the phone and try to sleep, but I don't and I can't.

Australia 218, Lee 47; SP Jones 5-44, Hoggard 3-70; and 222-4 (following on), Langer 61, Ponting 48; Flintoff 2-33. England lead by 37 runs.

Day four

In the fitful night I wait and I hope, wait and hope that the anaesthetic will wear off, and that when it does, the feeling will be bearable. It's false hope though, and it's crushed the minute I try to get up. I put weight on the ankle and fall over. I can't even touch the floor with it. I grab the phone and dial Kirk's room.

'Mate, I can't walk. I need some crutches or something.'

He's non-committal.

'Kirk, come to the room.'

He sees in my face that I'm badly distressed. He gets me some breakfast and takes me to the ground, but the atmosphere is awful again. I feel as if I've let the lads down. I'd backed myself to get through the game, promised that I would, and I haven't. It's demoralising. It hurts, badly. Vaughany's still not talking to me. I understand that it's not deliberate, but it doesn't help.

Australia bat well. Clarke and Katich get half centuries. Bloody Warnie gets 45. He's made more than some of the batsmen this summer. Lee gets another 26. They get a lead; they pass 350; they eke out every run. They end up with 387.

We need 129 to take a 2–1 lead in the Ashes.

The game will end today, one way or another. I'm not sure at which point it dawns on me that I may have to bat, but the thought of it crowds my mind. I'll be allowed a runner. What's worrying me is how I'll get from the Pavilion to the field of play. I'm concerned that I'll be timed out.[7]

Tres and Strauss open. All of the pressure that has been on Australia is now on us. The door is open, but we still have to walk through. They have nothing to lose that's not almost gone already and they know it.

The best way to approach short chases is to play freely, break the back of the opposition before they can get a grip on you. Tres starts with a blaze of boundaries. After five overs the score is 32 and the target already under a hundred. Lee is bowling

---

[7] The Laws of the game state that an incoming batsman must take guard or be ready at the non-striker's end within three minutes of the fall of the preceding wicket. A player can be given out on appeal if not. No batsman has ever been timed out in Test cricket and there have only been five instances in the first-class game. However, with the Ashes on the line, I didn't want to test the theory.

as fast as he has all series. Ponting keeps him on and calls for Warne – his two big guns, his two last hopes.

Warne has been here many times before, the ball in his hand and his country needing something – anything – from him. He gestures to the umpire that he will come around the wicket. He and Ponting set the kind of field you might see on a raging fifth-day dustbowl in Mumbai. Smoke and mirrors.

He does Tres first ball, bat-pad to Ponting at silly mid-off. Sharp catch.

He does Vaughan with the first ball of his second over, caught by Hayden at slip from a leading edge.

He does Strauss with the fifth ball of his fourth over, caught by Clarke at leg slip from the face of the bat.

Brett Lee does Ian Bell two balls later, caught by Kasper at fine leg on the hook.

From nowhere, from the safety of our harbour, the score is 57-4.

Shane Warne. Brett Lee. Doubt and fear where there was hope and expectation. The atmosphere in the ground is indescribable. Every run is being cheered as if it's the winning hit. Every wicket brings a sort of chill, the chill that has accompanied eighteen years of failure, eighteen years of *this*. There is a low, electric hum that never quite stops. The dressing room is a mess, kit everywhere, people padding up, people stripping down. Those of us that can watch sit still and quiet. Those that can't pop up and down. Vaughan's like a meerkat. Harmi is giggling. The only reason I'm sitting down is because I really can't move.

Fred and Kev push them back. Everything now is heightened.

Every ball is a rocket, a bomb. Fred whooshes his second delivery in the air through backward point for four. Shaun Tait bowls a viciously quick bouncer that Kev top edges over Gilchrist for four more. They scrabble singles, sprinting hard.

Warne wants to tempt them, draw the big shot, but they resist.

The big shots come at the other end, against Shaun Tait. Kev flicks him to the fine leg boundary then smokes one through midwicket. Warne throws one so high Fred can't ignore it and he hits it well over the infield for four more. The noise of the crowd when he does means we can't hear each other speak, not that anyone's got anything sensible to say.

We're almost there now, we can nearly breathe. The hundred comes up. Lee comes back with 27 needed. Ponting's last gunslinger.

Lee does KP with the first ball of his first over, a big drive that he edges to Gilchrist.

Lee does Fred with the fourth ball of his second over, an unplayable jaffa that pitches on middle and hits the top of off at more than 90 mph.

Warne does Geraint in the next over, caught by Kasper at long-off from a fretful hoick.

We need thirteen runs. Australia need three wickets. The thirteen runs seem like the harder task. Harmi has put his pads on, so I get the boot off and put mine on too. I worry about the hopping. I worry about the runner. Harmi and I have nearly run each other out plenty of times without one.

Below us in the crowd, I see people hiding under their coats, unable to look at what's happening in front of them.

What's happening is this: Brett Lee is reversing it at 95 mph at one end. The greatest spinner in the history of the game is bowling at the other.

The batsmen are Ashley Giles and Matthew Hoggard.

I hear Freddie behind me, jumping around, telling stupid jokes. I look at Fletch, inscrutable behind his reflector glasses. Vaughan sits. Harmison sits. I sit. None of us can do anything about anything.

Hoggy squeezes three from a Lee over.

Ten needed.

Gilo works Warne through midwicket for two.

Eight needed.

Lee bowls Hoggy two short ones. He gets out of the way.

Lee goes for the yorker but he gets it ever so slightly wrong and the ball reaches Hoggy on the full. He gets the face of the bat on it and it rumbles through extra cover towards the rope. Everyone in the ground roars it on. Vaughany's leaning over the balcony watching it, fist pumping the air.

I think Hoggy just played the greatest shot of his life. What a man he is.

Four needed.

Please just let us get there...

Hoggy gets two more to fine leg.

Two needed.

The crowd are singing: 'BARMY ARMY, BARMY ARMY'. The rhythm drums in my head.

Australia are done now, surely...

Warne comes in to Gilo. The field is up. Gilo defends the first two. Warne bowls a full toss.

This must be it...Let this be it...

Gilo strikes it well, but it hits Katich at short leg.

Vaughany jumps up, and then hides behind a pillar.

Warne comes in again. He bowls a slider that misses off stump by a hair. Had it hit, I'd have been hopping down the stairs…

Warne comes in again, and this time Gilo gets the middle of the bat on it. It beats the field and Gilo and Hoggy clock up the two most beautiful runs they'll ever complete.

It's over. It's over at last. The relief is so strong and pure that it obscures any other feeling. We're hugging each other and laughing. All the pain and the doubt has gone, all of the weight and the pressure is lifted.

The Australians come in to us this time. They look like we feel. The atmosphere is different. It's more like two groups of mates chatting. Two teams that have played amazing cricket have a beer. I know now that they respect us. I know too how much we respect them. They may have lost, but they have not been beaten. With everything against them, they got close to pulling off the miracle.

I get lots of questions about my ankle, but Fletch has told me to play it down, so I tell them it's fine and I'll be ready for them at the Oval. Kirk's had a word too. I'm allowed to go out, but absolutely no booze. He says: 'We've got ten days to get that ankle right.'

It feels strange not drinking, but at least I'm with the lads.

Six hours later we're in some terrible nightclub with deafening music. Matty Maynard and Angus Fraser are having the biggest barney I've seen in my life. Apparently it's about Matt not feeling welcome when he first came into the England side. I can hear them shouting at each other over the top of some pounding deep house. I realise that I'm laughing. For the first time in a couple of days, I almost feel normal.

8. Money

'*Look, mate, we don't think you're going to make it back.*'

19 July 2009, Worcester. Steve Rhodes, Worcester-shire's coach, looks me in the eye as he delivers the news. I love Steve, I've loved my time at Worcester. I've won them plenty of games. They offered me a sanctuary and looked after me when I was at a low ebb.

My knee has gone again though, and the rest of 2009 is a write-off. My two-year deal is up at the end of the season.

Steve can make big decisions. He doesn't try to bullshit me. He doesn't bother with a silly offer that he knows I'll turn down. He gives it to me straight. They think I'm finished, or if I'm not, another rehab will last so long that it's too much of a risk to have me on the books. There's nothing for me here.

I am thirty years old, with my partner Justine and two young sons at home waiting for news. We've just bought a new house. It's a horrific feeling. I sit in the car and cry my eyes out. I don't know what to do. The thought of another rehab is breaking me up. We're eating into our savings.

Where do I go from here?

*

One of my first quick spells cost the Jones family money. When I bowled out Millfield School with Wales Under 15s, they offered me a scholarship. It was a big opportunity. The school's playing fields, in sight of Glastonbury Tor, had produced plenty of high-class sportsmen and Millfield was especially strong in rugby and cricket.[8] The facilities were outstanding: Somerset played a lot of their second XI games on the Millfield pitch, and the school cricket coach was a man with a ten-wicket haul in an Ashes Test, Richard Ellison.

Mum and Dad called a family meeting. Millfield's offer was for a 90 per cent scholarship, but the other 10 per cent was still a considerable amount for us. My brothers Math and Richard agreed to miss out on a few things so that I could go. Mum and Dad made their sacrifices and found the money. From that moment I knew that I'd use any cash that I made to repay them somehow.

I had my first pro contract before I left Millfield. I didn't think too much about money, certainly didn't worry about money. I thought about cars, bought a few that I shouldn't have. I looked after my mum and dad and my brothers; I enjoyed being able to pay for dinner or drinks when I was out with my mates.

I had been born at the right time. In my father's era, cricketers were working men. Once they retired from the game, their other life began. Some county players needed alternative employment during the off-season because contracts lasted

---

[8] Millfield was founded by a cricketer, Somerset's RJO Meyer. Amongst its cricketing alumni are Peter Denning, Peter Roebuck, David Graveney, Craig Kieswetter, Wes Durston, Rory Hamilton-Brown and Tom Maynard, Matt Maynard's late and much-missed son.

only six months. An England cap was rewarded with a simple match fee. My dad got no huge insurance payout when his career was ended by injury. At twenty-six he had to go out and do something else.

My fluke of birth meant that I came into the England side just as revenues from television rights were significantly altering the finances of the game around the world. The system of central contracts that Australia had implemented during their years of dominance was adopted by the ECB in 2000, two years before my debut. By relieving counties of the burden of paying the salaries of their best players, money began to flow through the top of the game. The Ashes series of 2005 opened further commercial opportunities for both the ECB, who had negotiated a new broadcast deal with BSkyB, and the players. T20 cricket, which began domestically in 2003, started new revenue streams for county cricket. The IPL began in 2008 with a player auction that created several overnight millionaires. The money-grab may have reached its nadir in the same year with a T20 tournament financed by Allen Stanford in which his 'Stanford Superstars' defeated an England XI for an apparent $1m per player,[1] but the point holds: the beginning of the new century was perhaps the first time in history that international cricketers might retire from the game having earned life-changing sums of money.

---

[1] Stanford was convicted of Wire Fraud in the US in 2012 and is serving a sentence of 110 years for running one of the biggest Ponzi schemes ever uncovered. Although his Stanford Superstars team were supposed to receive $1m each for beating England, some of the players are said to have reinvested the money with Stanford and then lost it after the company collapsed.

My winter in the new ECB Academy in Adelaide came with a fee of £15,000. My match fee on my England debut the following summer was £2,600. When I went to Australia in the winter of 2002–3 to play in the Ashes, my tour fee was £25,000. My annual contract with Glamorgan was another £40,000, so I was earning considerable sums for a young man, way more than any of my mates would see at the same age.

It was after the injury at Brisbane that the fragility of the professional sportsman's life first hit home. Had I been forced to retire, my insurance payout would have lasted me less than six months because I wasn't centrally contracted at the time.

However, the ECB paid out my full tour fee, and Glamorgan had to pay me through my rehab. I knew that I'd get back, but I could feel the pressure of it too. That's why I did everything the doctors and physios said, to the letter.

I got my first central contract in West Indies in 2004. They came in three bands: A, B and C. I began on a C contract, which was for £105,000 per year, with match and tour fees on top. After the Ashes of 2005, I moved to the B strand, which was between £140,000 and £150,000 per year. I had a good equipment contract with Puma, and a modelling deal with Jaeger. Life with England was full of perks and opportunities. All the time we were away we stayed in lovely hotels, ate the best food. Travel was business class. Everything we needed was taken care of. I remember we were each given one of the first picture messaging mobiles by a sponsor. The first image I got on mine, which involved Marcus Trescothick and the stomach bug that had been troubling him in India, has stayed with me for all of the wrong reasons.

I retained my central contract for another year after my second knee injury. I saved as much as I could. I bought my first house. I still had no idea of the pain that lay ahead.

There's a lasting perception that the 2005 team are all millionaires. Some are, and if that's the case, they've got there on the back of hard work. But some of us aren't. There was no automatic right, and while Kev, Ian Bell, Colly, Andrew Strauss, Fred and Harmi made it to the next home Ashes in 2009 and in some cases beyond, the side was never to play together again. Michael Vaughan's knee forced him into retirement. Fred's would do the same. Marcus Trescothick's difficulties cost him his international career. Geraint Jones lost his place. Gilo retired in 2006. It was an illustration of the transience of the sport.

There was a moment, in the weeks and months after the series, when the opportunities were there to capitalise on our fame. Fred was a national hero. Kev was a nascent superstar. Some of the lads published books, did media work and appeared in adverts. I was in a bad place though. All I was thinking about was getting back on a cricket field.

Kev said to me, 'Mate, why aren't you getting yourself out there?'

I didn't want to. I didn't want to go to openings or premieres, I didn't want my picture in celebrity mags. I was voted the ninth sexiest man in the world by *New Woman* magazine. It seemed absurd to me. The lads ribbed me about it and I joined in, but I was in the wrong frame of mind to embrace it all. Ultimately, it cost me money.

*

I lost my central contract towards the end of 2007. It hurt. I knew it was the end of something. It suggested that they thought I would not get back. It meant that Glamorgan were now responsible for paying my wages. I thought we had an understanding on what the salary would be should the situation arise, and, from my point of view, they let me down. In 2004, I'd had a very lucrative offer from Surrey, which I'd rejected. I felt I was due some loyalty.

At the end of 2007, I met with Matt Maynard, who had left England and was back at Glamorgan as a coach, and Mike Fatkin, the county's chief executive, in Cardiff. Their first offer was £20,000 plus appearance fees.

I actually laughed when Mike said it, but it felt like a knife in the guts.

He said, 'Okay, well £40,000 plus appearances,' and soon we got as far as £60,000, but by that point it wasn't about the money any more. It felt like they'd tried to shaft me.

I know now that what I really wanted, what I really *needed*, was simply for one of them to put an arm around my shoulder and say, 'Mate, we believe in you.' That would have been worth more than money to me. Instead it seemed like we were playing a stupid game of bargaining and one-upmanship.

I left the meeting and spoke to Steve Rhodes at Worcestershire. I knew that Steve liked me as a player. He offered me £80,000 right away, and beyond that he let me know how much he wanted me at the club.

I went back to see Mike Fatkin. I think he was expecting me to accept his offer.

'Mike, it's not good news. I'm off.'

His eyes seemed to sink into his head.

'Your first offer ended all negotiations for me. I was disgusted, really hurt.'

There was nothing more to say. Matt Maynard called as I was driving out of the ground. His voicemail message was very calm. He wished me all the best.

A mate of mine rang to tell me that all the pictures of me in the offices were being ripped down.

The Worcester deal bought me some time, but I worried about life after cricket. Richard Steadman had given me two years. He'd done hundreds of operations like mine and he knew. Instead of planning for it, I got stubborn and focused even more on cricket. I knew the truth of my situation but I didn't want to believe it. People were talking about the knee, whispering about me. I was doing the business out on the pitch, but I was bowling too much, eating into my remaining time just to prove a point to myself and to the world.

It was tough for Justine to be around me. She was dealing with two young boys, plus a partner who was rarely at home, and when he was, he was moody and self-obsessed. All of the perks had gone. The sponsors had drifted away. The contract was running out – and then the knee blew up again.

It was a horrific feeling when Steve Rhodes let me go. Justine wasn't working because the boys were still young. We had no money coming in. My management were searching desperately for a deal. I rang Rod Bransgrove at Hampshire. Rod is a wonderful man, a miracle worker who raised the Rose Bowl out of nowhere and made it into a Test match ground; whose vision helped to turn the county from 'Happy Hampshire' that never won into serial white-ball champions; who brought Shane Warne to the club to transform its mentality... and who helped me out when I really needed it.

Hampshire offered me a six-month pay-as-you-play contract. I took it. I let my management thrash out the detail. I needed something, *anything*, and this was a lifeline. It didn't occur to me that I would be putting myself under unbearable pressure to stay fit, although it should have been obvious. It was something I could go home and tell Justine about, some good news at last... I was still a cricketer.

I became obsessive about my fitness. Iain Bunnschwieler wanted me leaner and stronger and I was determined to fulfil his brief. I remember Christmas 2009. I wasn't really thinking about Justine or the boys and their holiday. I wasn't thinking about my and Math's birthday, which falls on Christmas Day. I was thinking about going to the gym as early as possible on Boxing Day, because I knew no one else would be training. I got down to 88 kilos with 6 per cent body fat. I looked like a ghost.

I had to leave Justine and the boys in Wales and move into a flat in Southampton that was costing £450 per month. I had nine hundred quid a month to live on. When the season began I discovered that the deal I'd signed had no guarantee of a contract at the end of it. The pressure was doubled, squared, cubed...

I wanted to prove everyone wrong. I became a person I no longer knew. When I look at photographs of myself from that summer, I don't recognise my face. I was entirely and totally lost.

The pressure to play was immense. When I bowled, I bowled fast – I was clocked at 94 mph – but I couldn't sustain it. The knee would swell and I would miss another couple of weeks.

I remember a T20 game at Canterbury where my knee was agony. I was thinking, 'It's okay, I'm hiding this quite well.' Then when I ran in I began to feel the knife-like pains I'd had before both operations.

I looked at Chris Wood at mid-on. I said, 'Mate, my knee's killing.'

He said, 'Well just stop.'

'Mate, I can't.'

When the lads were going out for beers, I couldn't go because the knee would swell up. If the knee swelled up, I couldn't play for two or three weeks, and I didn't get paid. I was too proud to say, and I didn't want to affect the harmony of the changing room, but the truth was that if I had a beer my wife and kids were directly affected.

Sometimes I'd think about my success in 2005, and wonder what I'd done wrong, who I'd offended.

My stubbornness, my desire to prove people wrong, cost us money. What was I doing paying £450 for a flat in Hampshire, when I had a house in Wales to maintain? How could I live on the £900 a month I was left with? By the middle of 2011 – the season that I'd planned for and trained to play in full-time – I wasn't in the Hampshire side. Glamorgan needed a bowler and I went back on a month's loan that they wanted to make permanent at the end of the season. At least it meant I could move back to Wales and be with Justine and my boys.

Glamorgan did the deal for two years, but even then for some reason or another, I wasn't paid for three months. They put a signing-on fee of £1,500 in my account and then took it back out again. I got payslips that read '£0.00'. For most of 2012 I played white-ball cricket. In 2013 we got through to the YB40 final, and I spoke to the club about some sort of Twenty20 deal.

Hugh Morris had returned to Glamorgan from the ECB as Chief Executive. Each week I would call and ask about the contract. Each week his secretary would tell me that he'd be in touch. I waited two months. When the call finally came, it was short and there was no offer.

I speak to Justine and say, with all we've been through as a couple, we can get through anything. What we've dealt with has been horrific. It's all character building, but some of the mistakes I've made . . . I'd like to turn back time. I wish I'd stopped in 2009 and begun coaching or something new. I'm still close with Steve Rhodes at Worcester, with Rod Bransgrove at Hampshire, with Matthew Mott at Glamorgan, but I've learned some hard lessons. There's a great value in that, and I believe that I'm a better person for it. I need to work. I need to find a path in life beyond cricket. I need to wipe away those four years in which I lost sight of myself.

Justine is an unstoppable force, a businesswoman, an inspiration to me. My boys are everything. I'm a lucky man, I know that.

*

But rich? Nah, not me, bud. Not yet, anyway… Though if I had a quid for everyone who thought I was a millionaire, I'd be a millionaire by now…

9. The Oval

In which I get a reality check, encounter strange faith, join the nation in having our nerves shredded and end up in a hotel room with a strange man…

The hyperbaric chamber at the Wellington hospital looks like a beached submarine. Cold, cast iron with an air-sealed door. Portholes for windows. Two rows of small, hard seats inside.

Pure oxygen delivered at high-pressure improves the body's ability to heal itself. The chamber helps to dissolve oxygen into all body fluids, including blood plasma, central nervous system fluids, lymph and bone. It's especially effective in soft tissue traumas. It can get athletes back on the field four or five days quicker. It's why I'm here.

It's not why the man with gangrene in his foot is here though. Or the cancer patients who are trying to heal skin reactions caused by radiotherapy. Or the other very ill people who share these hard seats with pillows provided by the nurses and sit for the three hours per session, unable to do anything other than wave at the faces in the portholes asking if everything is okay, and flip through books and magazines to kill the time. Once the chamber is sealed and pressurised, it's like being on a flight in a very small plane. No one's getting out.

We smile and nod, but there's not much else to say. They have real problems that they didn't ask for or choose, and that they may not survive. I'm worried about whether I can run up and bowl in a cricket match.

It's a sobering place to be, a jolt of sad reality in a summer that had become heightened and obsessive. I'm not sure how I feel about being here. I'm doing it because I've been asked to, and I'll try anything that may get me out on the field at the Oval, but in my heart I know it's over. It hurts to walk around.

As soon as the Trent Bridge Test was finished, I went into a pretty bad place. The thing that scared me most was waking up on the final morning of the game and not being able to put my foot on the floor. It felt like someone slipping a knife into the ankle and working it up and down. There's something bad going on inside it. I've been living on painkillers. I've had three cortisones, plus local anaesthetic.

Kirk says another jab is pointless: 'If you're in this much pain so soon after the other one, it's not going to touch it.'

So instead there is oxygen, anti-inflammatories, painkillers, massage. Then will come exercise in a therapeutic swimming pool with gradation at the bottom that allows more and more weight to be added slowly while exercising. A couple of days before the game comes, D-Day, I will try and run for the first time.

*

Kirk's face keeps appearing at one of the portholes. He gurns and grins and tries to keep my spirits up. He's a special bloke. He has huge pressure on him to get us all fit. He has a couple of masseurs to help him, but it's a big job. But I can see even Kirk starting to lose faith. I feel frustrated and robbed somehow – everyone else will play in all five Tests and have the chance to finish the job. We've worked together, sweated together, stuck together against the best team in the world, and now I won't get to be there at the end, and it's deeply frustrating. I got five wickets in the first innings at Trent Bridge when I was 75 per cent fit. What could I have done at 90 per cent, or 95? I've taken eighteen wickets in three and a half Tests. How many could I have got? I turn it over and over in my mind as I sit in the chamber, and then I think, 'Yes, but I don't have cancer. I don't have gangrene.' I have no right to feel sorry for myself. I've no problems, not real problems. Just those that belong to the unreal world of pro sport.

I suck at the air and count down the minutes...

Duncan tells the press conference that he's 'not confident' I'll recover. Discussions about who'll replace me gain traction. Chris Tremlett's been in the squad all summer. I'd like to see him get a game, but Chris is a six feet seven bang-it-in bowler. I think he'd be more likely to be chosen if Harmi were out. Jimmy Anderson is a like-for-like replacement as a swing bowler, but Fletch seems to favour Paul Collingwood who will strengthen the batting in a game we only need to draw. He can bowl some useful overs too, and he's probably the best fielder in England.

I know what Fletch really wants though, and that's me fit. Or at least not unfit. The same eleven for a whole summer.

The game is all anyone seems to talk about, which makes it tough too. Cricket has gripped England in a way that it hasn't in many years, probably since 1981.[1] The TV ratings are overwhelmingly high. The papers are full of cricket, front and back. I get recognised in the street every day, especially in London. It should be wonderful – it is wonderful – and yet I am already beginning to feel distant from it.

Ricky Ponting is fined 75 per cent of his match fee, around £4,000, for shouting at Fletch after he was run out at Trent Bridge. Simon Katich is fined 50 per cent of his match fee, £2,600, for arguing with the crowd when he was dismissed in the second innings.[2] Gillespie has had a moan about the crowds, too. The unease they feel is bubbling up all the time now.

Ponting issues an apology for his behaviour and acknowledges that I had a genuine reason to be off the field. He continues to complain about our use of substitutes. He's still stewing about the basic principle.

---

[1] The series for ever known as Botham's Ashes, when England recovered from a seemingly impossible position while following on in the third Test at Headingley, led by the great all-rounder's 149. Botham had been captain for the first two Tests, but with England trailing 1–0 and having made a pair in the second match at Lord's he'd been sacked in favour of Mike Brearley. A spell of 5–1 inspired another unlikely win in the next Test at Edgbaston, and then his magical 86-ball century at Old Trafford in the fifth saw England take an unbeatable 3–1 lead in the series. Botham took ten wickets in the draw in the sixth and final Test at the Oval. I was only three, I looked this up.

[2] England and Australia's players were almost all centrally contracted. It's usual to receive a match fee on top of the contract's basic salary as a part of the overall deal.

Vaughan defends the bowlers. 'They have to take on a lot of liquid.'

The phoney war rumbles on. Australia play another two-day game, this time at Essex. Neither McGrath nor Warne appear. McGrath bowls at half-pace in the warm-ups. Warne is stiff and sore after a summer of sweat and grind. John Buchanan concedes that his future will be in doubt if Australia lose the Ashes. Ponting is being pressured too.

Gilo, Ian Bell, Chris Tremlett and Kev are released to play for their counties in the final of the C&G Trophy at Lord's. Kev and the Hampshire boys are in the same hotel as me. They go to Lord's. I go to the Wellington for my oxygen treatment. Hampshire win. Gilo gets Kev out, much to his delight. The squad is named the next day, a Sunday. Jimmy Anderson and Paul Collingwood are in. Chris Tremlett is out. I have until Tuesday to prove my fitness. McGrath declares himself fit for Australia. They call up Stuart Clark again anyway. All of these things are discussed endlessly, in the papers, on the radio, in the pubs…

The hyperbaric chamber sessions finish. I move on to the swimming pool, which is at a Premier League football club. The lads there are obsessed by the cricket too. They ask about my chances.

'Maybe…' I say.

Kirk has one more roll of the dice.

'Horse, would you be willing to see a faith healer?'

'Mate, I'll try anything…'

She comes to my hotel room that evening. Kirk brings her

up. She speaks to me in a gentle voice. She asks Kirk to leave. He goes with a massive smile on his face.

I think, 'Mate, what are you doing to me?'

She puts her hands around the ankle. After a while she says, 'Can you feel any heat?'

I can't. I dunno what to say. I don't like to upset her.

'Yeah, it's a little bit warm.'

Well, who really knows? Maybe it'll feel hot later. I'll take anything at this stage.

The fitness test comes the next day. Kirk and I go back to the football club, out onto the grass training pitches. We start running. Within four or five yards I know.

'Kirk, it's no good...'

'No, mate,' he says. 'We've got to keep going, see if it eases at all.'

'All right, mate,' I say wearily, 'let's have a crack then.'

We have a couple of twenty-metre sprints. A forty-metre sprint.

'Sorry, Kirk,' I say.

'No, come on, Jonah. A couple more...'

'No point, mate, I'm done.'

The next twenty minutes are hard. Kirk's put so much into this. So have I. We both want it so badly, but I feel the truth in every step, and there's no hiding from it. We sit in silence on the grass. I'd been trying not to delude myself, but there's always a part of you that thinks, 'It's not feeling right but you never know...'

Well now I know. Kirk knows. We go to the Oval to let everyone else know. All I can think of in the car on the way there is, 'What am I going to do for the next five days?'

As a team we'd promised each other we'd get through the series together, and now we wouldn't. They'd be sweating and toiling out on the field, and I can only watch them do it.

At the ground, Kirk talks to Fletch and Michael Vaughan, and they tell the lads. Fletch pulls me aside. 'Get yourself back home for a couple of days,' he says. 'Have some rest, clear your head and come back when the game's started.'

I understand why he's saying what he's saying. He needs complete focus from the group for the biggest game of their lives and having someone around who is not involved can be a distraction, especially if their mood isn't great. I get it, and I'll abide by it, but I would love to have stayed and been useful, maybe take the mitt in practice and help out, throw balls, knock catches, whatever.

I chat to a few press guys – can't remember what I say – and take a look around the ground. The team head back to practice. They're instantly absorbed in it, seeing nothing other than what they're doing. The circle closes around them. I watch from the outside what I have been inside for so long.

I head home. The house is empty. I mooch around, wonder what I'm going to do with myself for three days. Although I don't entirely agree, now I'm here, I see the wisdom of Fletch's choice. At least I'm free to feel exactly how I want to feel without it affecting anyone else. I can allow the disappointment and frustration to run through me and not worry about how it makes me look or what it makes me say.

In the end it's my dad who finds the right words.

'Si, you've had an amazing series. You've done everything

you possibly can do to try to get fit. You've got nothing to blame yourself for. So relax, have a few beers, and when you get back down, enjoy being part of whatever happens.'

I text the boys, one by one. I wish them all the best. I tell them I'm okay, and they just need to do what they've been doing all through the series, and I'll see them in the changing room on day three. I know from the messages I get back that it's appreciated. The guy who misses out should always make the first move.

My mate Chris turns up, along with Erj. We have those beers. I feel the buzz and I realise that it's the first time all summer I've started to relax. I'm not thinking about my prep, worrying about the ankle; not sweating over where to bowl to Ricky Ponting, or why the ball's not coming out how I want it to. It's only once the weight has lifted that I realise how heavy it was.

It's still there though, just at a different level. In my head now is the make up of the team, the genius of Warne, the flatness of the Oval wicket...Nerves and doubts, but not my nerves, not my doubts, not any more.

Day one

It's hard to watch. That's what I discover on the first morning of the final Test. I'm in and out of the room, up and down on the sofa, wondering about the toss, mithering about it, who'll win it, who'll do what...

England win the toss. Vaughan bats first. As I watch it happen I realise I never usually see any of this, Mark Nicholas standing there with the two captains, a camera up their noses, watching the coin go up, hearing the call and who's won and who's doing what. I'm usually on the massage table, sweating on what happens, listening as Andrew Flintoff puts 'Rocket Man' on the boombox for the one hundredth time this summer.

I should be there. I should be there with the boys, listening to 'Rocket Man', going out on the field . . . except for this shitty little injury . . . out on that park.

Thoughts I find impossible to stop.

Never played a Test at the Oval. Never played in a one-dayer at the Oval. One wicket where I'd really like to have a go, test myself . . . especially against that lot . . .

Strauss and Trescothick open up against Glenn McGrath and Brett Lee. Paul Collingwood has taken my place. Australia have dropped Kasprowicz. The first hour goes to England, as it has done in each of the four preceding Tests. At the first drinks break, fourteen overs have been bowled, and the score is 71-0. Trescothick has hit Lee for consecutive boundaries. Strauss has hit McGrath for consecutive boundaries.

Lee has been replaced by Tait. Strauss has hit Tait for two boundaries in his second over. McGrath has been replaced by Warne. Strauss and Trescothick both hit him for four in his first over.

On television, the Oval outfield looks huge and flat. The ball seems to travel over it differently when it's mediated by the screen. The noises are different when they come through microphones. The full angle is narrowed to the width of the pitch. It's not as if I never watch cricket on television, but today it seems to emphasise the distance between me and the team.

Even the sound of the crowd, so all-encompassing, and the theme tune to my summer, is contained, muted.

I play with the volume, distracted. I want to know what's happening, but I don't want to watch.

The game shifts as quickly as my mood. Strauss belts the first ball after drinks for four. Warne has Tres caught at slip by Matty Hayden. Vaughany goes in and right away pulls Warne for four and drives him for another. Then he plunks another short one straight to Clarke at short midwicket. Bell goes in and Warne gets him for nought, leg before wicket, absolutely plumb. Kev goes in and makes ten from his first five deliveries from Shaun Tait. They walk off for lunch.

I imagine the happy clatter, Harmi and Hoggy delighted to get their grub.

I'm up and down, in and out...the rest of the afternoon blurs by...

Kev goes soon after lunch, bowled by Warne, who seems to have decided to win the Test and save the Ashes on his own. Fred goes in. Even through the glaze of television, it's obvious that something has happened: the crowd love him, absolutely love him. The commentators do too. He's at the centre of the great narrative arc that they've developed, offering heroics in every Test. The dressing-room insecurities and idiosyncrasies, the things that we know so well and love him for, don't show up on screen. In their place is this giant blond god, a hero in whom everyone places their faith, their hope.

Fred does something that no one quite expects. He bats quietly until tea, taking his time, giving Strauss the strike. It's only after the break that he opens up. He hits Warne for three consecutive boundaries to get to fifty. Either side of that little onslaught, Strauss clips a couple of fours that take him to a hundred, his second of the series. Fred hits Lee for a couple more boundaries. He carts Warne for six over midwicket. McGrath comes back. Fred nicks off to Warne at slip for 72. Paul Collingwood goes in. He bats for half an hour until Rudi Koertzen gives him the finger of death when he's hit on the boot by Shaun Tait. Warne gets Strauss for 129, caught at bat pad by Simon Katich. Geraint Jones and Ashley Giles bat until the close.

England 319-7, Strauss 129, Flintoff 72; Warne 5-118.

Day two

I travel to London. The weather is heavy, the air thick and humid beneath huge, late-summer rainclouds. I catch only fleeting glimpses of a day's cricket that goes against the pattern of the rest of the series. We fall short of 400 on first innings for the first time since Lord's. Jonah goes early to Brett Lee, bowled at off stump. Hoggy gets gnarly and digs in. He takes thirty deliveries to get off the mark. Gilo scores well at the other end. McGrath gets Hoggy with a slower ball that he slaps to Damien Martyn at cover. Harmi hits Brett Lee for three fours in a row, much to Lee's delight. Warne gets Gilo leg before wicket with a slider. England 373 all out. Not quite 400. Not a score that shuts Australia out of the game. Not a score that makes it easy for them either.

Langer and Hayden go in just before lunch and for the first

time this summer they ride the early overs. Langer gathers pace. He hits Gilo for consecutive sixes. Haydos digs in. For the first time this summer they put on a hundred together. For the first time this summer, Haydos gets to thirty and then doesn't get out. Instead, when the light deteriorates at tea, when the giant thunderheads tower over the south of the city, in a Test match Australia have to win, they take the umpires' offer and walk off for the day.

England 373 all out, Strauss 129; Warne 6-122; Australia 112-0, Langer 75 not out.

Day three

The third day of the final Test is another equivocal day. The weather forces long interruptions. The struggle is slow, a trial of strength and endurance now. Cloudbursts punctuate dense heat. Langer and Hayden bat and bat. The lads toil before them. Australian runs weigh heavily on the huge, murmuring crowd. I sit out on the balcony. If being away from the ground was strange, being there is just as unsettling. The team is focused and intense, inside the bubble, shutting out distraction. They have their jobs to do. I have no job except to sit. Kirk has told me to rest for two weeks minimum. Probably longer. Then we'll make a decision as to whether or not to operate on my ankle. We have winter tours to Pakistan and India for me to make.

There's no television screen between us any more, but there is still that separation. I feel part of things but not, because I'm not out there where I should be, sharing the load, shouldering my burden. I want to be here and I don't.

In the end, it's as close as I can get to going through it with them.

Three hours of play take six hours to complete in the rain and the light. Langer survives a close leg-before shout first ball. Hayden and Langer survive run-out chances. Hayden survives another good leg-before shout. Just before the first downpour, Langer goes to a hundred with an edgy boundary from Steve Harmison, who is bowing quickly and without luck. Langer cuts another over the slips. Harmi looks at the darkening heavens and throws one out wide. Langer, perhaps loose after the boundaries and the arrival of his hundred, chops it down into his stumps.

The players take lunch and then tea while the rain falls. It feels slightly more normal once the dressing room is full again.

They go back out, the light clear and grey, the clouds building again in the distance. Two hundred and eighteen deliveries after he started batting, Hayden ends his summer nightmares with a mishit drive down the ground for four and then a better-struck on-drive for another to raise a century. At no point has he seemed fluent, or anything like the marauding Haydos of old, but like all great players he has found a way. Fred goes over to congratulate him. Ponting looks even more pleased than Hayden. A few balls later, the rain comes down again.

The dressing room fills and then empties. The weather opens up enough for Flintoff to bowl another mighty spell. How he has laboured for us. He flogs the ball into the wicket and the extra bounce takes Ponting's glove and loops to gully, where

Strauss dives forwards to catch it. Fred then hurries Damien Martyn until he's forced to take the light for the final time.

England 373; Australia 272-2, Hayden 110 not out, Langer 105; Flintoff 1-47. England lead by 96 runs.

Day four

Australia are behind but they are ahead. They know it and we know it. That's a paradox of the game. For the first time since Lord's they have runs on the board and wickets in hand. They have a five-man attack reduced to four. They have a flat wicket and a maximum of 196 overs left in the match, ninety-eight per day.

Sunday, just like Friday and Saturday, is a day of dull light and occasional rain, but the forecast is for everything to improve. We may have to bat for a long time to save the game and win the Ashes.

John Buchanan has had his calculator out. He says they'll bat another ninety overs, look to lead by 250 to 300 and then bowl. All of a sudden it sounds like the old Australia – telling the world what they will do, and then doing it.

Only today they will not, they will not do it because once again this summer Andrew Flintoff will stand up, stand up in the morning gloom of the Oval and wrench this game from their grasp. With the fourth ball of his second over, he surprises Damien Martyn with a ball of steepling bounce that Martyn tries to pull but simply swats high into the sky, from where it drops into the waiting hands of Paul Collingwood.

The clouds build up once more. Rudi Koertzen reads his meter and offers the light to Matthew Hayden and Michael Clarke, who tell him that they want to stay on. Haydos picks up his big bat and drives Hoggy for a couple of boundaries. Clarke gets Flintoff away. Hoggard comes off and Harmison replaces him. Hayden pulls Harmison for four. An over after drinks, Australia are just fifty runs behind.

Flintoff seizes the ball. He runs in harder than ever and a booming inswinger thuds into Hayden's front pad. Three hundred and three deliveries Hayden has faced, and this one is too good for him. Rudi raises the slow finger.

With the sixth ball of his eighth over, Fred brings the ball back into Katich from a full length and has him leg-before too. Rudi raises the slow finger of death.

I watch the crowd. It's as if Flintoff has stirred this wild thing into life.

Matthew Hoggard stands up. With the first ball of the fifth over of his spell, he brings the ball back into Adam Gilchrist, who plays all around it. Billy Bowden raises the crooked finger.

Lunch comes. I sit out by the steps on a big body-ball. There are a couple of girls who work for Red Stripe looking over. They smile. Usually I'd smile back, but not today. One of them says, 'He looks miserable.'

With the third ball of his sixth over, Hoggard gets Clarke with the straight one again. It clips his pad bang in front. Billy Bowden raises the crooked finger.

With the fifth ball of Flintoff's next over, he rams the ball into the pitch again, and Shane Warne can only send it miles up into the air, where it drops into the hands of Michael Vaughan.

With the sixth ball of his seventh over, Hoggard has McGrath caught at second slip by Andrew Strauss.

With the first ball of his eighth over, Hoggard has Brett Lee caught in the deep by Ashley Giles.

So much for a lead of 250. So much for having ninety overs to bowl England out. Astonishingly, from a score of 281-2 they are finished and done on 367. Eight wickets gone for 86 runs in 28.3 overs.

England lead by six runs. Flintoff has bowled unchanged for eighteen overs. If he wasn't a legend already, he is now.

The Australians must be stewing, dark, sick, fucking sick about this.

The series almost done, the Ashes almost gone.

One more chance for them ... one last hope ... ten very quick wickets and knock off the runs ...

England bat for 13.2 overs, ducking on and off the field as the grey light flickers. Shane Warne comes into the attack after three overs, just before another stoppage. With his third delivery he turns a giant leg-break from the edge of the cut strip back towards Strauss's pad. It flicks to Katich from the inside edge.

When the umpires deem the light to be playable again, a marginal decision, the entire Australian team return to the field in sunglasses.

England 373; Australia 367 all out, Hayden 138, Langer 105; Flintoff 5-78, Hoggard 4-97; England second innings 34-1, Vaughan 19 not out; Warne 1-14. England lead by 40 runs.

Day five

The longest day of all begins in sunshine (at last). Can't sleep, can't eat, coffee tastes like mud. All of the lads are the same. We have been working for four years towards this day. I think of those who have fallen by the wayside – Graham Thorpe, Mark Butcher, Darren Gough. Great players who played a whole career against Australia without a day like this one: Mike Atherton, Alec Stewart; Nasser, my first captain, who began it all with Fletch. I think of our promise to one another before we started the cycle of our last five series: to go unbeaten against West Indies, New Zealand, South Africa, Bangladesh and Australia.

Tres, Vaughany, Gilo, Fred and Harmi have been there all the way. Kev and Belly and Colly are fighting with us now. One more day. One day away.

How long can we bat? How long against McGrath and Warne, Lee and Tait?

How many runs do we need to be safe? Safe from Langer and Hayden, Ponting and Martyn, Clarke and Gilchrist?

As he has done so often this summer, Vaughan feels the mood and finds the words. 'Lads... What's going on? Just bat. Do what we've done for four and a half games. Christ almighty, it's simple. Why are we thinking outside the box? Get out there and enjoy it.'

There's nothing I can do to help, but that doesn't feel quite as difficult to handle today, because there's not much I can do with the bat anyway. I find my big comfy chair out on the balcony and watch the ground fill until everywhere I look people are sitting shoulder to shoulder under the September sun. Over the gasholders the skies are clear as far as the eye can see, mile upon mile of spotless blue.

Tres and Vaughany go out.

Warne has four deliveries of last night's final over to finish. The second of those is a full-toss that Vaughany whacks to the fence. In Brett Lee's first over, he guides another to the third-man boundary. In Glenn McGrath's first over, he gets him away through third man too. In McGrath's second over he hits a classical off-drive that jerks sections of the Oval to its feet.

Ten overs pass without alarm, ten overs that begin to lull the early nerves, and then it happens, then it comes.

Glenn McGrath is all healed up and has his rhythm today, has his snap and his power, and he has a wicket that he likes, a wicket with pace and bounce from a good length.

Vaughan feels for the third ball of his ninth over and edges it low towards first slip. Gilchrist dives across and pouches it inches from the ground.

An end opens... the nerves return.

Ian Bell goes out. McGrath's first ball to him bounces and takes a regulation edge. Shane Warne holds the catch.

Three wickets gone now. Three wickets down, and McGrath on a hat-trick at the Oval. An Ashes hat-trick...

Kev goes in. Behind me, people who had been sitting calmly are grabbing for kit, strapping on pads.

McGrath's hat-trick ball is brutal. Four or five mph quicker than anything he's bowled in a month, rising almost vertically from the wicket to shoulder height. Kev tries to ride it but at the last second realises he won't be able to and jerks his gloves out of the way. The ball hits something and flies to Ponting who catches it and runs towards Billy Bowden, waving it in the air.

And Billy, bloody beautiful Billy, just shakes his head and keeps his crooked finger in his pocket, despite the deflection, despite the imploring shouts of Ponting and Warne, McGrath and Gilchrist, despite the hat-trick ball and the Ashes on the line.

It's a brilliant decision. The dressing-room television replays show the ball missing Kev's gloves and brushing his shoulder in a blur of movement that played out in fractions of seconds.

McGrath smiles... Ponting smiles... they knew...

They know that they're in this game too, right back in this game. After almost four matches of being dominated, they can still take it away from us at the last, take it away as legends do.

The pre-lunch period becomes a lurching psychodrama in which neither side will back down.

Kev is hot-wired on adrenaline. He pulls McGrath for four through midwicket. Tres edges Warne past slip. McGrath comes off and Lee comes on. Kev drives his first ball straight back past him for four. Lee stays full and Kev drives the third to cover, and then tries to smack the fourth through mid-off but gets a big nick that flies at head height to Shane Warne at first slip. He drops it.

Never seen Warne do that before. He pulls his sunhat over his face.

Maybe he's still shaken when he bowls his next over because Kev hits the first and last deliveries for six. Not just a little way over the rope either. Right into the Oval stands, huge carries on both.

I'm still watching, but I don't know how. Kev and I have got close this summer. It feels as if I'm watching my brother play, that same slightly sick feeling.

Warne the champion digs deep. He forgets about the drop and the sixes and turns one back into Trescothick, a big ripping leggie that Rudi adjudges will hit the stumps. Up goes the slow finger of death, as unwelcome today as it was glorious yesterday.

Fred goes in. This time there are no heroics. Warne beats him in the flight and he pops back a simple catch. Warne doesn't drop this one, and it's a nightmare, a bloody nightmare just before lunch.

I don't know if anyone eats. I don't, or if I do I don't remember it. Kev changes his shirt. In the over before lunch, Lee hit him in the ribs and then on the gloves with a ball timed at 93.7 mph. He's still there though. I think, 'Kev, this is your chance, pal. You've got to take this.'

They go back out. This session will decide the summer, one way or another. Us or them.

Lee bowls like the wind from the Pavilion End, the ball almost invisible from the balcony ninety yards away.

Kev takes him on. He pulls the fourth ball of his first over miles into the crowd.

Lee fires up even more. Kev hooks the third ball of his next over way beyond square leg. Lee goes short and and Kev hits it like a bullet, low and flat and one bounce past Shaun Tait at long-leg. Lee goes full and on leg stump, and Kev glides him to the ropes again. The big screen shows 96.7 mph.

The crowd are out of their seats and out of their heads. The roars must be audible all over London. This is astonishing, him-or-me cricket. I realise that this *is* Kev's moment. He's shown glimpses of his ability all summer. Others would be cowed by the magnitude of what is happening, but Kev thinks, 'I'm going to be me…I'm going to enjoy it.' He has the pure balls to do it, too. I think of Rod Marsh at the Academy: 'He's the best since Ponting…'

Ponting gees Lee up. He surrounds Paul Collingwood as he faces Shane Warne. He turns the screw.

Kev wins the battle with Brett. No one can keep bowling at that pace for ever. Kev senses his chance, and smashes the fifth ball of his next over through extra cover. Lee gives it one last go, another short one, and Kev hits his pull-shot so early it scorches back past the bowler, hitting the fence before he's finished his follow through.

Lee comes off and McGrath comes on.

Ponting needs something now. The lead is 177. There are a maximum of sixty-six overs left in the day, minus two for the change of innings. Sixty-four overs.

How many more can we bat?

How many more runs do we need before the lead is too big for them to chase down? We soak up seven more overs before Warne has Colly caught at bat pad by Ricky Ponting. He has resisted for almost two precious hours, a heroic effort of self-denial.

Geraint goes in. They play calmly for four overs. McGrath goes off and Tait comes on. Kev slaughters his first ball through cover for four and his second through point for four more. He knocks a single and then Tait bowls Geraint with a 90 mph reverse swinging yorker.

Gilo goes in. The lead is 202. Kev has 90. The atmosphere in the dressing room has shifted along the scale from sick nerves towards excitement. We are nearly there. Even Kev reins back as his first Test hundred comes close. He pings Tait for four. He pushes Warne for a single. He pushes Tait for another. Gilo blocks out an over from each.

Come on, mate.

Tait bowls him a half-volley that he creams straight to mid-on. The crowd groan. Kev taps the wicket, head down. The next is wide and full and he thrashes it through extra cover. He runs down the pitch pumping his fist as the crowd suck the ball over the rope.

What an innings. What a player. He could go his whole career and never bat under this sort of pressure again. He went in on a hat-trick ball with everything on the line and he got a hundred . . . that's special.

His hair is still ridiculous though. The white skunk is back, and when he pulls off his helmet, it's glued to his head like it's been run over.

Four balls later they walk in for tea. It's the happiest interval of our lives.

Australia are defeated but not beaten. They take it like champions. They stretch themselves to the last, even though Kev is making merry with the bowling and Gilo is resisting and resisting, making sure that the last chink of light is extinguished.

Kev launches a joyous last assault. He hooks Lee for six, and then, two deliveries later, smacks Warne for another. He goes from 142 to his 150 in consecutive deliveries, lifting Warne for six more and then scorching him through point for four.[3]

The mayhem ends soon afterwards, when McGrath squares him up and knocks back his off stump. As Kev walks off, Warne does a remarkable thing. He runs across to shake his hand and tells him: 'Enjoy this, mate…' He understands the fleeting nature of moments like this one, and doesn't want it to pass Kevin by.

Kev spins around and sees everyone in the ground on their feet.

The end becomes chaotic. Gilo reaches fifty with back-to-back boundaries from Warne. There could be no one better to be there at the finish; our gatekeeper, our unsung hero. Warne produces one more big leg break and bowls him.[4] Two balls later, he turns another across Harmi's bat and Hayden takes the catch. [5]

I watch it all with a massive smile on my face. It's the most pleasurable cricket I've ever seen.

---

[3] Kev's innings of 158 contained seven sixes, a new Ashes record. In all, he batted for 187 deliveries, and hit fifteen fours along with the maximums.

[4] Gilo's 59 was his highest Test score. And it still is, as he didn't manage to top it before he retired in 2006.

[5] Warne's stats for match and series were remarkable. He had match figures of 12-246, and a series total of 40 wickets at an average of 19.92. In addition he made 249 runs at 27.66, with a top score of 90.

Australia need a nominal 342 from eighteen overs. We stand at the top of the steps and hug Gilo as he comes off. We are keeping a lid on our feelings, but release is close.

Australia go in. Harmi bowls a speed-of-light bouncer at Langer, and the umpires immediately offer the light. Hayden and Langer walk off. The game is not over, because the light could improve, but this is England in September so it ain't gonna happen. The covers go on.

Rudi walks into the dressing room.

'It's done,' he says, and we're hugging and cheering and going nuts. The relief is utterly overwhelming, and it consumes me. Lord's seems like a lifetime ago, not six and a bit weeks.

No one really knows what to do, whether we should go back out or not. We just want it over so we can lift that precious urn, celebrate with the crowd and get more pissed than we have ever been in our lives.

It's an anti-climax when it comes. After all of the crazy finishes we've had, the series ends when Rudi Koertzen and Billy Bowden are cheered to the middle of the Kennington Oval so that they can symbolically lift the bails from each set of stumps and declare the fifth and final test a draw.

The presentation blurs past. We all take a turn at lifting the urn. We all go nuts. The walk around the ground moves me almost more than anything else. There are people hugging, crying, embracing, laughing, kissing, just because of something we've done. It's an amazing feeling, probably indescribable beyond saying how rarely it comes.

An hour or so later we're in the rooms, the ground emptying

at last. We're already well into the beers when Phil Neale comes in.

'Right lads, quick chat,' he says.

'Fuck off, Nealo...'

'No lads, seriously. You've got a bus tour tomorrow morning.'

Fred lets out a huge laugh. 'Where? What time?'

'Half nine. The Lord Mayor's Mansion House, Ten Downing Street, Trafalgar Square and Lord's...'

Fred spits his beer halfway across the room.

'You're joking...'

'No lads, it's serious,' says Vaughany. 'It's happening. They just didn't want anyone knowing before the game. Well, not the oppo...'

The Australians come in soon afterwards. We swap shirts, and sign some stuff for one another. My respect for them is total. I get a shirt from Brett and one from Kasper. I ask Matty Hayden for one of his, but they've already gone. Warnie's have gone too. What a legend he has been. I give some of mine out. We sit and talk, all marvelling at the series we have played in. They're experienced enough as players to realise its value, even though their disappointment must be tearing a hole in their hearts. We've all been part of something that can never be repeated.

Fred and Harmi prop up the bar back at the hotel. They're well into a serious session and I join them for a while, but then there's a clamour to head out to some place called the Cabaret Club, so I do. Later I'll wish I'd stayed behind with those two and just reflected on everything that had happened, talking and drinking with them through the night, but I don't. Instead I'm going nuts in this club with the rest of the lads and a bunch of people I don't know, and the moment passes. For once Fred and Harmi had the right idea.

I don't remember getting back to the hotel but evidently I have. It's past breakfast time. Somehow I get into my suit and tie for the parade thing. I can't find my sunglasses though and it's a bloody bright morning and the sun is like a knife through the brain. Then I see Fred and he looks like a Cyclops, which makes me feel somewhat better.

No one knows whether anyone will come and see this bus. It's a working day, we're all hammered and we look as bad as we feel, but within a few minutes of setting off I realise that something extraordinary is happening. Every street is lined with people. Others are hanging out of windows and climbing lamp posts. No one seems to be at work. Even though I'm drunk, it's humbling and moving. All of these people who want to be part of something, a collective experience that has to happen right here, right now, before reality returns and splits us all up into our separate lives.

There's a hell of a lot of alcohol on this bus too, and we're drinking it...I know the only thing that can possibly keep me upright is more booze. Kill or cure. The first stop at the Mayor's official residence has these jugs of beer, and Kev and I take them back to the bus as they are, no glasses.

We're pretty far gone by the time we walk through the door of Number Ten. This place I've seen on TV so many times. Tony Blair is standing just inside, waiting. Thirteen extremely pissed cricketers shake his hand. God knows what he's thinking. I expect it's something like, 'Whose idea was this…?'

The house is huge, room upon room. We get a tour and then someone takes us out into the garden, which is quite beautiful. There's a table full of drinks, but they're non-alcoholic, orange juice, lemonade, water. Vaughany, as captain and leader, grabs the nearest waiter.

'Look, mate, sort some beers and wine quick will you…?'

By the time it transpires that the 'waiter' is actually Tony Blair's eldest son Euan, Harmison is on the climbing frame and Fred is on the swing.

This could be a PR disaster. There must be sixty photographers in the garden for a start.

Tony Blair comes out.

'What do all these photographers want?' he asks.

Matthew Hoggard says, 'A photograph, you knob.'

Within minutes we leave 10 Downing Street.

Trafalgar Square is full of people. We march onto a long stage in front of the National Portrait Gallery. 'Jerusalem' is playing. Mark Nicholas comes along the line, asking each of us a question. Fred lifts his sunglasses and the crowd cheers rapturously. Mark gets to me. As he does, I see the horror in his eyes as he realises how drunk I am. All I can say is, 'WE DUN'EM…' which barely makes sense even to me, but the crowd cheers anyway. Mark Nicholas moves quickly away.

The bus takes us to Lord's. We do something or other there – I remember sitting on some benches out on the field, but I'm wilting badly. It's almost 4 p.m. It'd be a long day for the sober, let alone men who've now been awake for thirty hours. At last they put us onto another bus, a lovely, comfortable one with air conditioning and huge seats. Fred finds a couple of bottles of champagne at the back. He opens both, pours them down his throat and collapses. As he sleeps, Harmi finds a marker pen from somewhere. He writes the word TWAT across his forehead and on both cheeks.

The bus takes us to another hotel, the City Grange near Tower Bridge. It's a lovely place. We stagger through the doors. The reception is buzzing with guests and visitors. Flintoff wakes up and walks in. People are laughing at him, but he can't work out why. He stumbles over to the lifts, which have full-length mirrors beside them. He stares at himself for a minute while his brain slowly absorbs what's scrawled on his face, then he whirls around and begins chasing Harmison. We bundle them into the lifts before they can hurt anyone.

I get to my room. I start to take off my trousers and make the fatal mistake of sitting on the bed. I wake up sixteen hours later in exactly the same position, flat on my back, trousers round my ankles. Someone is in the bed behind me.

'Oi…' I say.

Gary Pratt's head peeks out over the covers.

'Sorry, mate, they didn't give me a room, so I kipped here.'

So, I think, this is how it ends…

10. Unbreakable

*'*H*ey, mate, it's Bryan. Listen, I've just met a girl…she's really nice…'*

It's a few months after the Oval Test. My ankle's been cleaned up, I'm feeling good. I'm out somewhere or other and the mobile goes. It's Bryan Pietersen, Kev's brother. We've become good mates over the summer. Bryan has the same kind of confidence that Kev has at the crease, except he has it when he's out on the town…

'Good for you, Bry,' I say. 'I'm happy for you.'

'No no, listen, she'd be perfect for you. I'm going to give you her number.'

'Mate, if this is a wind-up…' I can imagine him laughing as he sets me up with his next-door neighbour's granny or something.

'Nah, it's no wind-up. I met her in this restaurant and we got talking. She's Welsh. And she doesn't know who you are…'

Her name's Justine. I arrange to take her out in Cardiff. I decide on Pizza Express. If it is one of Bry's wind-ups, at least it won't be an expensive date.

We go out and Bryan's right. She makes me laugh all through our cheap dinner. I have a great time.

'Hey,' she says. 'I remember you now. I've seen you before, you know.'

'Oh yeah, where's that then?'

'At the Oval. Me and my mate were doing PR for Red Stripe. We were on the stairs by the dressing room. You were sitting on this big gym ball looking moody…'

Some things are just meant to be.

It's hard to believe that those five Ashes Tests were a decade ago. It feels like yesterday, but also half a life. So much has happened. Time has offered a new perspective on them. The matches themselves remain dreamlike, their climaxes scripted – except no writer would dare to make them up for fear of not being believed. After every game, the players of both sides would sit together looking slightly shell-shocked and drained by the drama, and wonder what would happen next. The cricket reached a rare height because neither team was prepared to back down or surrender its principles. The combination of skills and personalities was perfect. Because of the schedule, the series was condensed into a few weeks. There was no down time for the drama to ebb away. It was the last series to be on free-to-air television in the UK. Two nations became entirely caught up in it. In so many ways it was a perfect storm, one that has come rarely in the long history of the game.

The comedown was hard, for me personally, and for the

team. In light of the subsequent 5–0 defeat in Australia eighteen months later, the celebrations in Trafalgar Square and the other awards and presentations were seen as an overreaction. Now I feel they're viewed differently, as the passing of time demonstrates just how rare that series was. It's an old cliché, but cricket was the winner – those celebrations were not just of the win, but of the game and its power to entertain.

The Trent Bridge Test was my eighteenth and last. That still seems unreal, and amazingly unlucky. Sometimes I'm asked if I would trade having played in 2005 for a career of forty or sixty Test matches that didn't include a series like that one. Perhaps when I was struggling to come back, I would have said yes. But now – no way. Not for the world. To have played then was to have played when the game was about as good as it's going to get, against opponents who were legends of the sport and who have my total respect. If that was the bargain I had to make, then I would make it again.

A couple of summers ago I ran into Ricky Ponting. We were chatting away when he said: 'Mate, you know I used to have nightmares about facing you. We had team meetings that were just about how to play you.'

It was one of the greatest compliments of my life. To know that I had the respect of one of the all-time great batsmen and of his team is a wonderful feeling. On the field we went at one another as hard as we could. We had our moments. But from it grew an enduring bond.

*

The team of 2005 took four years to build. If we had stayed together I believe we may have been able to dominate for three or four more seasons. Instead, the twelve of us went away to our different, separate futures.

I think the defeat made Shane Warne and Glenn McGrath determined to carry on for another eighteen months and win the Ashes back. Revenge was a dish best served cold. Nine of their 2005 eleven started the first Test in Brisbane in November 2006; by the time they had completed the whitewash of England, Justin Langer, Damien Martyn, Warne and McGrath had announced their retirements.

English cricket was torn apart after that 2006 defeat. I felt for Fred, who was under almost unbearable strain as captain. Fletch's time as coach ended in rancour that he did not deserve. But from that defeat came a new side that took three of the next four Ashes series, including that yearned-for victory in Australia in 2010–11. Australia entered a reckoning of their own as the last of the legendary generation left the team: Hayden and Gilchrist in 2009, Ponting in 2012. The series of 2005 changed a dynamic that had existed for two decades.

The other question I'm often asked is: What was the sledging like?

I can barely think of any. I've mentioned most of it. The teams were so bound up in trying to get the better of one another, no one had the time or the energy to waste.

In the New Year's honours list of 2006, Fletch and Vaughany

were awarded OBEs and the rest of us MBEs.[1] We were allowed to bring two guests to the Palace for the investiture, so I took my mum and dad.

The Queen came over to us. She'd been amazingly well briefed. She walked straight up to my mum and said, 'Ah, Mrs Jones, you must be very proud.' It made my mum's day, and probably her year too.

I was so worried about getting the protocol right – knowing when to bow, and how long to stand there while the Queen made the presentation – that I don't really remember much about it, but it was a very special day for our family. The medal now resides with my mum and dad – I can't be trusted with it.

A while later, I was able to take my dad to the *Wisden* dinner after I'd been voted one of the Almanack's five Cricketers of the Year for 2006. That was another proud moment. It's an accolade that began in 1889, and outstanding players from WG Grace and CB Fry to Brian Lara and Sachin Tendulkar have been recognised. It is only awarded once in a career. The other four players named in my year were Matthew Hoggard, Kevin Pietersen, Brett Lee and Ricky Ponting, so I have some pretty decent names to share it with.[2]

---

[1] Paul Collingwood's MBE did attract some famous sledging at the Sydney Test in 2007, when a stump mike picked up Shane Warne asking him: 'You got an MBE right? For scoring seven at the Oval?' Colly laughed it off, and as the rest of his career showed, he has been as worthy a recipient as any of a sporting honour: a multiple Ashes winner and captain of England's World T20 winning side.

[2] Steve Harmison, Ashley Giles, Andrew Strauss and Marcus Trescothick were named on the 2005 list, along with Rob Key. Vaughan had been named in 2003 and Andrew Flintoff in 2004.

These things mean more to me as time goes by.

That first date with Justine marked the end of my single, lad-about-town life. I knew that I'd met the right person for me. She was there with me through the most difficult times, keeping everything together. Our son Harvey was born in November 2006, and Charlie came along in April 2008, so there's a new generation of Jones boys playing sport in the garden and being overcompetitive in everything from cricket to board games. I see a lot of my own spirit in them, and I'm trying to teach them how to handle it. I've certainly got the experience – and the scars to prove it.

Justine became Mrs Jones in December 2011. She still gives me stick about taking her to Pizza Express, though.

In retrospect there were several moments when I should have given up the struggle to play that was driven by the relentless 'what if' question in my head. At least I'll never have to answer that. Even at the very end, I hung on. Glamorgan reached the YB40 Final at Lord's, and that could have been my sign-off. But we waited and waited to see if a new deal would come along. Every week, either Justine or I would ring the club to see if they'd made a decision. Those were eight weeks of uncertainty that seemed symbolic of the previous four years. When that call came from Hugh Morris, it cut the ties I'd had in my heart for the club my dad had played for, where I began at sixteen. It will never be the same for me there now.

And yet the relief was massive. I hadn't realised the amount of stress I was under until it was gone. I didn't have to wake up in the morning consumed by thoughts of my knee, or training, or pain or money. My body began to feel better almost right away. The scary thought, however, was, 'What do I do now?' I've still not fully answered that question, but we're working it out.

I can still bowl quick, somewhere in the mid-80s, from a few paces, just not for very long. I still dream about cricket too, and in my dreams I'm bowling really fast, like I used to, but this time in a big final somewhere. The game is still in my subconscious, and there bowling fast is pain-free and exhilarating, like it used to be.

And I wake up and think back to those days when it felt like flying.

APPENDIX:
Ashes 2005 Scorecards

England v Australia – 1st Test
Lord's Cricket Ground, London – 21–25 July 2005
Australia wins the toss and elects to bat

Australia 1st innings		R
JL Langer	c Harmison b Flintoff	40
ML Hayden	b Hoggard	12
RT Ponting*	c Strauss b Harmison	9
DR Martyn	c †GO Jones b SP Jones	2
MJ Clarke	lbw b SP Jones	11
SM Katich	c †GO Jones b Harmison	27
AC Gilchrist†	c †GO Jones b Flintoff	26
SK Warne	b Harmison	28
B Lee	c †GO Jones b Harmison	3
JN Gillespie	lbw b Harmison	1
GD McGrath	not out	10
Extras	(b 5, lb 4, w 1, nb 11)	21
Total	**(all out; 40.2 overs; 209 mins)**	**190**

Bowling	O	M	R	W	Econ	
SJ Harmison	11.2	0	43	5	3.79	
MJ Hoggard	8	0	40	1	5.00	(2nb)
A Flintoff	11	2	50	2	4.54	(9nb)
SP Jones	10	0	48	2	4.80	(1w)

England 1st innings   R

ME Trescothick	c Langer b McGrath	4
AJ Strauss	c Warne b McGrath	2
MP Vaughan*	b McGrath	3
IR Bell	b McGrath	6
KP Pietersen	c Martyn b Warne	57
A Flintoff	b McGrath	0
GO Jones†	c †Gilchrist b Lee	30
AF Giles	c †Gilchrist b Lee	11
MJ Hoggard	c Hayden b Warne	0
SJ Harmison	c Martyn b Lee	11
SP Jones	not out	20
Extras	(b 1, lb 5, nb 5)	11
Total	**(all out; 48.1 overs; 227 mins)**	**155**

Bowling	O	M	R	W	Econ	
GD McGrath	18	5	53	5	2.94	
B Lee	15.1	5	47	3	3.09	(4nb)
JN Gillespie	8	1	30	0	3.75	(1nb)
SK Warne	7	2	19	2	2.71	

Australia 2nd innings

		R
JL Langer	run out (Pietersen)	6
ML Hayden	b Flintoff	34
RT Ponting*	c sub (JC Hildreth) b Hoggard	42
DR Martyn	lbw b Harmison	65
MJ Clarke	b Hoggard	91
SM Katich	c SP Jones b Harmison	67
AC Gilchrist†	b Flintoff	10
SK Warne	c Giles b Harmison	2
B Lee	run out (Giles)	8
JN Gillespie	b SP Jones	13
GD McGrath	not out	20
Extras	(b 10, lb 8, nb 8)	26
Total	**(all out; 100.4 overs; 457 mins)**	**384**

Bowling	O	M	R	W	Econ	
SJ Harmison	27.4	6	54	3	1.95	
MJ Hoggard	16	1	56	2	3.50	(2nb)
A Flintoff	27	4	123	2	4.55	(5nb)
SP Jones	18	1	69	1	3.83	(1nb)
AF Giles	11	1	56	0	5.09	
IR Bell	1	0	8	0	8.00	

England 2nd innings R

ME Trescothick	c Hayden b Warne	44
AJ Strauss	c & b Lee	37
MP Vaughan*	b Lee	4
IR Bell	lbw b Warne	8
KP Pietersen	not out	64
A Flintoff	c †Gilchrist b Warne	3
GO Jones†	c Gillespie b McGrath	6
AF Giles	c Hayden b McGrath	0
MJ Hoggard	lbw b McGrath	0
SJ Harmison	lbw b Warne	0
SP Jones	c Warne b McGrath	0
Extras	(b 6, lb 5, nb 3)	14
Total	**(all out; 58.1 overs; 268 mins)**	**180**

Bowling	O	M	R	W	Econ	
GD McGrath	17.1	2	29	4	1.68	
B Lee	15	3	58	2	3.86	(1nb)
JN Gillespie	6	0	18	0	3.00	(2nb)
SK Warne	20	2	64	4	3.20	

Australia wins by 239 runs

England v Australia – 2nd Test

Edgbaston, Birmingham – 4–8 August 2005

Australia wins the toss and elects to field

England 1st innings		R
ME Trescothick	c †Gilchrist b Kasprowicz	90
AJ Strauss	b Warne	48
MP Vaughan*	c Lee b Gillespie	24
IR Bell	c †Gilchrist b Kasprowicz	6
KP Pietersen	c Katich b Lee	71
A Flintoff	c †Gilchrist b Gillespie	68
GO Jones†	c †Gilchrist b Kasprowicz	1
AF Giles	lbw b Warne	23
MJ Hoggard	lbw b Warne	16
SJ Harmison	b Warne	17
SP Jones	not out	19
Extras	(lb 9, w 1, nb 14)	24
Total	**(all out; 79.2 overs; 356 mins)**	**407**

Bowling	O	M	R	W	Econ	
B Lee	17	1	111	1	6.52	(3nb, 1w)
JN Gillespie	22	3	91	2	4.13	(3nb)
MS Kasprowicz	15	3	80	3	5.33	(8nb)
SK Warne	25.2	4	116	4	4.57	

Australia 1st innings   **R**

JL Langer	lbw b SP Jones	82
ML Hayden	c Strauss b Hoggard	0
RT Ponting*	c Vaughan b Giles	61
DR Martyn	run out (Vaughan)	20
MJ Clarke	c †GO Jones b Giles	40
SM Katich	c †GO Jones b Flintoff	4
AC Gilchrist†	not out	49
SK Warne	b Giles	8
B Lee	c Flintoff b SP Jones	6
JN Gillespie	lbw b Flintoff	7
MS Kasprowicz	lbw b Flintoff	0
Extras	(b 13, lb 7, w 1, nb 10)	31
Total	**(all out; 76 overs; 346 mins)**	**308**

Bowling	O	M	R	W	Econ	
SJ Harmison	11	1	48	0	4.36	(2nb)
MJ Hoggard	8	0	41	1	5.12	(4nb)
SP Jones	16	2	69	2	4.31	(1nb, 1w)
A Flintoff	15	1	52	3	3.46	(3nb)
AF Giles	26	2	78	3	3.00	

England 2nd innings

		R
ME Trescothick	c †Gilchrist b Lee	21
AJ Strauss	b Warne	6
MJ Hoggard	c Hayden b Lee	1
MP Vaughan*	b Lee	1
IR Bell	c †Gilchrist b Warne	21
KP Pietersen	c †Gilchrist b Warne	20
A Flintoff	b Warne	73
GO Jones†	c Ponting b Lee	9
AF Giles	c Hayden b Warne	8
SJ Harmison	c Ponting b Warne	0
SP Jones	not out	12
Extras	(lb 1, nb 9)	10
Total	**(all out; 52.1 overs; 249 mins)**	**182**

Bowling	O	M	R	W	Econ	
B Lee	18	1	82	4	4.55	(5nb)
JN Gillespie	8	0	24	0	3.00	(1nb)
MS Kasprowicz	3	0	29	0	9.66	(3nb)
SK Warne		23.1	7	46	6	1.98

Australia 2nd innings		R
JL Langer	b Flintoff	28
ML Hayden	c Trescothick b SP Jones	31
RT Ponting*	c †GO Jones b Flintoff	0
DR Martyn	c Bell b Hoggard	28
MJ Clarke	b Harmison	30
SM Katich	c Trescothick b Giles	16
AC Gilchrist†	c Flintoff b Giles	1
JN Gillespie	lbw b Flintoff	0
SK Warne	hit wicket b Flintoff	42
B Lee	not out	43
MS Kasprowicz	c †GO Jones b Harmison	20
Extras	(b 13, lb 8, w 1, nb 18)	40
Total	**(all out; 64.3 overs; 307 mins)**	**279**

Bowling | O | M | R | W | Econ |
--- | --- | --- | --- | --- | --- | ---
SJ Harmison | 17.3 | 3 | 62 | 2 | 3.54 | (1nb, 1w)
MJ Hoggard | 5 | 0 | 26 | 1 | 5.20 |
AF Giles | 15 | 3 | 68 | 2 | 4.53 |
A Flintoff | 22 | 3 | 79 | 4 | 3.59 | (13nb)
SP Jones | 5 | 1 | 23 | 1 | 4.60 |

England wins by 2 runs

England v Australia – 3rd Test
Old Trafford, Manchester – 11–15 August 2005
England wins the toss and elects to bat

England 1st innings		R
ME Trescothick	c †Gilchrist b Warne	63
AJ Strauss	b Lee	6
MP Vaughan*	c McGrath b Katich	166
IR Bell	c †Gilchrist b Lee	59
KP Pietersen	c sub (BJ Hodge) b Lee	21
MJ Hoggard	b Lee	4
A Flintoff	c Langer b Warne	46
GO Jones†	b Gillespie	42
AF Giles	c Hayden b Warne	0
SJ Harmison	not out	10
SP Jones	b Warne	0
Extras	(b 4, lb 5, w 3, nb 15)	27
Total	**(all out; 113.2 overs; 503 mins)**	**444**

Bowling	O	M	R	W	Econ	
GD McGrath	25	6	86	0	3.44	(4nb)
B Lee	27	6	100	4	3.70	(5nb, 2w)
JN Gillespie	19	2	114	1	6.00	(2nb, 1w)
SK Warne	33.2	5	99	4	2.97	(2nb)
SM Katich	9	1	36	1	4.00	

Australia 1st innings

		R
JL Langer	c Bell b Giles	31
ML Hayden	lbw b Giles	34
RT Ponting*	c Bell b SP Jones	7
DR Martyn	b Giles	20
SM Katich	b Flintoff	17
AC Gilchrist†	c †GO Jones b SP Jones	30
SK Warne	c Giles b SP Jones	90
MJ Clarke	c Flintoff b SP Jones	7
JN Gillespie	lbw b SP Jones	26
B Lee	c Trescothick b SP Jones	1
GD McGrath	not out	1
Extras	(b 8, lb 7, w 8, nb 15)	38
Total	**(all out; 84.5 overs; 393 mins)**	**302**

Bowling	O	M	R	W	Econ	
SJ Harmison	10	0	47	0	4.70	(3nb)
MJ Hoggard	6	2	22	0	3.66	
A Flintoff	20	1	65	1	3.25	(8nb)
SP Jones	17.5	6	53	6	2.97	(1nb, 2w)
AF Giles	31	4	100	3	3.22	(1w)

England 2nd innings   **R**

ME Trescothick	b McGrath	41
AJ Strauss	c Martyn b McGrath	106
MP Vaughan*	c sub (BJ Hodge) b Lee	14
IR Bell	c Katich b McGrath	65
KP Pietersen	lbw b McGrath	0
A Flintoff	b McGrath	4
GO Jones†	not out	27
AF Giles	not out	0
Extras	(b 5, lb 3, w 1, nb 14)	23
Total	**(6 wickets dec; 61.5 overs; 288 mins)**	**280**

Bowling	O	M	R	W	Econ	
GD McGrath	20.5	1	115	5	5.52	(6nb, 1w)
B Lee	12	0	60	1	5.00	(4nb)
SK Warne	25	3	74	0	2.96	
JN Gillespie	4	0	23	0	5.75	(4nb)

Australia 2nd innings		**R**
JL Langer	c †GO Jones b Hoggard	14
ML Hayden	b Flintoff	36
RT Ponting*	c †GO Jones b Harmison	156
DR Martyn	lbw b Harmison	19
SM Katich	c Giles b Flintoff	12
AC Gilchrist†	c Bell b Flintoff	4
MJ Clarke	b SP Jones	39
JN Gillespie	lbw b Hoggard	0
SK Warne	c †GO Jones b Flintoff	34
B Lee	not out	18
GD McGrath	not out	5
Extras	(b 5, lb 8, w 1, nb 20)	34
Total	**(9 wickets; 108 overs; 474 mins)**	**371**

Bowling	**O**	**M**	**R**	**W**	**Econ**	
SJ Harmison	22	4	67	2	3.04	(4nb, 1w)
MJ Hoggard	13	0	49	2	3.76	(6nb)
AF Giles	26	4	93	0	3.57	
MP Vaughan	5	0	21	0	4.20	
A Flintoff	25	6	71	4	2.84	(9nb)
SP Jones	17	3	57	1	3.35	

Match drawn

England v Australia – 4th Test

Trent Bridge, Nottingham – 25–29 August 2005

England wins the toss and elects to bat

England 1st innings		R
ME Trescothick	b Tait	65
AJ Strauss	c Hayden b Warne	35
MP Vaughan*	c †Gilchrist b Ponting	58
IR Bell	c †Gilchrist b Tait	3
KP Pietersen	c †Gilchrist b Lee	45
A Flintoff	lbw b Tait	102
GO Jones†	c & b Kasprowicz	85
AF Giles	lbw b Warne	15
MJ Hoggard	c †Gilchrist b Warne	10
SJ Harmison	st †Gilchrist b Warne	2
SP Jones	not out	15
Extras	(b 1, lb 15, w 1, nb 25)	42
Total	**(all out; 123.1 overs; 537 mins)**	**477**

Bowling	O	M	R	W	Econ	
B Lee	32	2	131	1	4.09	(8nb)
MS Kasprowicz	32	3	122	1	3.81	(13nb)
SW Tait	24	4	97	3	4.04	(4nb)
SK Warne	29.1	4	102	4	3.49	
RT Ponting	6	2	9	1	1.50	(1w)

Australia 1st innings		R
JL Langer	c Bell b Hoggard	27
ML Hayden	lbw b Hoggard	7
RT Ponting*	lbw b SP Jones	1
DR Martyn	lbw b Hoggard	1
MJ Clarke	lbw b Harmison	36
SM Katich	c Strauss b SP Jones	45
AC Gilchrist†	c Strauss b Flintoff	27
SK Warne	c Bell b SP Jones	0
B Lee	c Bell b SP Jones	47
MS Kasprowicz	b SP Jones	5
SW Tait	not out	3
Extras	(lb 2, w 1, nb 16)	19
Total	**(all out; 49.1 overs; 247 mins)**	**218**

Bowling | O | M | R | W | Econ |
:--- | :--- | :--- | :--- | :--- | :--- | :---
SJ Harmison | 9 | 1 | 48 | 1 | 5.33 | (3nb)
MJ Hoggard | 15 | 3 | 70 | 3 | 4.66 | (4nb)
SP Jones | 14.1 | 4 | 44 | 5 | 3.10 | (1nb)
A Flintoff | 11 | 1 | 54 | 1 | 4.90 | (8nb, 1w)

Australia 2nd innings (following on) | | **R**

JL Langer	c Bell b Giles	61
ML Hayden	c Giles b Flintoff	26
RT Ponting*	run out (sub [GJ Pratt])	48
DR Martyn	c †GO Jones b Flintoff	13
MJ Clarke	c †GO Jones b Hoggard	56
SM Katich	lbw b Harmison	59
AC Gilchrist†	lbw b Hoggard	11
SK Warne	st †GO Jones b Giles	45
B Lee	not out	26
MS Kasprowicz	c †GO Jones b Harmison	19
SW Tait	b Harmison	4
Extras	(b 1, lb 4, nb 14)	19
Total	**(all out; 124 overs; 548 mins)**	**387**

Bowling	O	M	R	W	Econ	
MJ Hoggard	27	7	72	2	2.66	(1nb)
SP Jones	4	0	15	0	3.75	
SJ Harmison	30	5	93	3	3.10	(1nb)
A Flintoff	29	4	83	2	2.86	(9nb)
AF Giles	28	3	107	2	3.82	
IR Bell	6	2	12	0	2.00	(3nb)

England 2nd innings		**R**
ME Trescothick	c Ponting b Warne	27
AJ Strauss	c Clarke b Warne	23
MP Vaughan*	c Hayden b Warne	0
IR Bell	c Kasprowicz b Lee	3
KP Pietersen	c †Gilchrist b Lee	23
A Flintoff	b Lee	26
GO Jones†	c Kasprowicz b Warne	3
AF Giles	not out	7
MJ Hoggard	not out	8
Extras	(lb 4, nb 5)	9
Total	**(7 wickets; 31.5 overs; 168 mins)**	**129**

Bowling	**O**	**M**	**R**	**W**	**Econ**	
B Lee	12	0	51	3	4.25	(5nb)
MS Kasprowicz	2	0	19	0	9.50	
SK Warne	13.5	2	31	4	2.24	
SW Tait	4	0	24	0	6.00	

England wins by 3 wickets

England v Australia – 5th Test

The Oval, London – 8–12 September 2005

England wins the toss and elects to bat

England 1st innings		R
ME Trescothick	c Hayden b Warne	43
AJ Strauss	c Katich b Warne	129
MP Vaughan*	c Clarke b Warne	11
IR Bell	lbw b Warne	0
KP Pietersen	b Warne	14
A Flintoff	c Warne b McGrath	72
PD Collingwood	lbw b Tait	7
GO Jones†	b Lee	25
AF Giles	lbw b Warne	32
MJ Hoggard	c Martyn b McGrath	2
SJ Harmison	not out	20
Extras	(b 4, lb 6, w 1, nb 7)	18
Total	**(all out; 105.3 overs; 471 mins)**	**373**

Bowling	O	M	R	W	Econ	
GD McGrath	27	5	72	2	2.66	(1w)
B Lee	23	3	94	1	4.08	(3nb)
SW Tait	15	1	61	1	4.06	(3nb)
SK Warne	37.3	5	122	6	3.25	
SM Katich	3	0	14	0	4.66	

Australia 1st innings		R
JL Langer	b Harmison	105
ML Hayden	lbw b Flintoff	138
RT Ponting*	c Strauss b Flintoff	35
DR Martyn	c Collingwood b Flintoff	10
MJ Clarke	lbw b Hoggard	25
SM Katich	lbw b Flintoff	1
AC Gilchrist†	lbw b Hoggard	23
SK Warne	c Vaughan b Flintoff	0
B Lee	c Giles b Hoggard	6
GD McGrath	c Strauss b Hoggard	0
SW Tait	not out	1
Extras	(b 4, lb 8, w 2, nb 9)	23
Total	**(all out; 107.1 overs; 494 mins)**	**367**

Bowling	O	M	R	W	Econ	
SJ Harmison	22	2	87	1	3.95	(2nb, 2w)
MJ Hoggard	24.1	2	97	4	4.01	(1nb)
A Flintoff	34	10	78	5	2.29	(6nb)
AF Giles	23	1	76	0	3.30	
PD Collingwood	4	0	17	0	4.25	

England 2nd innings R

ME Trescothick	lbw b Warne	33
AJ Strauss	c Katich b Warne	1
MP Vaughan*	c †Gilchrist b McGrath	45
IR Bell	c Warne b McGrath	0
KP Pietersen	b McGrath	158
A Flintoff	c & b Warne	8
PD Collingwood	c Ponting b Warne	10
GO Jones†	b Tait	1
AF Giles	b Warne	59
MJ Hoggard	not out	4
SJ Harmison	c Hayden b Warne	0
Extras	(b 4, w 7, nb 5)	16
Total	**(all out; 91.3 overs; 432 mins)**	**335**

Bowling	O	M	R	W	Econ	
GD McGrath	26	3	85	3	3.26	(1nb)
B Lee	20	4	88	0	4.40	(4nb, 1w)
SK Warne	38.3	3	124	6	3.22	(1w)
MJ Clarke	2	0	6	0	3.00	
SW Tait	5	0	28	1	5.60	(1w)

Australia 2nd innings   **R**

JL Langer	not out	0
ML Hayden	not out	0
Extras	(lb 4)	4
Total	(0 wickets; 0.4 overs; 3 mins)	4

Bowling	**O**	**M**	**R**	**W**	**Econ**
SJ Harmison	0.4	0	0	0	0.00

Match drawn

England wins the series 2 v 1

Acknowledgments

I've encountered many people over the course of my career, and I'd like to acknowledge in particular the following for the roles that they played: Rod Marsh was a huge influence on me as a player and a person. He brought me out of my shell and gave me masses of confidence. He's one of the best people I've met. Duncan Fletcher saw my potential as an international player and backed me to the hilt. Fletch is a tough, honest man and I benefitted enormously from his knowledge of the game. Troy Cooley has been like a big brother. He never let me down, and he was always there when I needed him. A genius as a bowling coach, but more than that, a best mate! At Glamorgan Jeff Hammond, like others, saw my potential, and his integrity and honesty helped my emergence as a genuine quick bowler. When I went to Worcester, Gareth Batty became a true friend. We have very similar characters, and he never stopped making me laugh, even during the tough times. When I toured the West Indies in 2004 after coming back from my first serious injury, Mark

Butcher mentored me, supported me, and we became as thick as thieves. He's the most genuine person that anyone could meet – love you Butch!! Kevin Pietersen kept in constant touch during my roughest times, and is a true friend. He's sometimes misunderstood by the media and public, but never by me – I have immense respect for Kev. My four great friends Matthew Hoggard, Steve Harmison, Ashley Giles and Andrew Flintoff – the bond we formed as a bowling unit can never be broken. I'm proud to have taken the field with you. Erjan Mustafa was there when I needed the support and help required to get back to the England team – a best mate, my best man and I'm forever grateful. Kirk Russell is an all-round legend. He's as honest as the day is long, and he always stuck by me and supported me. Thanks Kirk. At Hampshire I'd like to thank Rod Bransgrove, Andrew Nealon, Brunchy and all of my teammates. I loved my time there, and also at Worcester, especially Bumpy Rhodes, Damien D'Oliveira, Ben Langley, Ben Davies and everyone I played with.

To my doubters: thanks for giving me the inspiration to look you in the eye when I proved you wrong! And thanks to all of the brilliant fans and followers whose endless love and support inspired me to carry on when maybe I shouldn't have.

This book focuses on the summer of 2005. To our lads, I'd like to say what a year, what a family and what memories. I always smile thinking about the fun – on and off the field!

To the Australians: what an honour to face what I consider to be the best team ever to have played the game. You were the toughest opponents by a mile, you brought out the best in me, and you were legends off the field too…

Thanks are also due to my agent Charlie Campbell, the entire team at Yellow Jersey Press including editor Matt Phillips, copy-editor Myra Jones, designer James Jones and publicist Laura Sherlock and of course to Jon Hotten, without whom there would be no book! Thank you to Will Hewitt and everyone at the Celtic Manor resort, especially the 2010 Clubhouse, who looked after us during the writing of the book.

Finally to my family: your undying love, support and honesty made me the person that I am today. Without you, who knows where I'd be. After the smooth came the rough but you never doubted me. If Carlsberg did families – well, enough said! Thank you Mum, Dad, Math, Rich and Dawn, Graham and Liz, Ronnie; and of course Justine and the two greatest achievements of my life, Harvey and Charlie.

INDEX

SJ indicates Simon Jones.